DEAR FELLOW

Spender

Enjoy Using
Your Money to
Get Out of Debt,
Build Savings, and
Create a Life You Love

EMILY BURNETT

Paperback ISBN-13: 979-8-9886775-0-5 Ellis Lane Press First Edition, July 2023. Updated 2025.

To my friends who know what it's like to stress about money.
Financial calm and abundance really can be yours.

Disclaimer

All names of clients and prospective clients in this book have been changed. In some cases, only incomplete information about their situation is provided to ensure client privacy.

The information provided in this book is for educational purposes only and should not be considered as professional financial advice. The author is not a licensed financial advisor, accountant, or lawyer and the content of this book is based on personal experiences. The reader should always consult with a licensed professional before making any financial decisions. The strategies and techniques discussed in this book may not be suitable for everyone and the reader should use their own judgment when deciding which strategies to implement. The author and publisher are not responsible for any financial outcomes that may occur from applying the methods suggested in this book.

Contents

Moso, pronounced "mo-so", is a type of bamboo. Like all bamboo, it grows slowly at first and largely invisibly while it's getting its roots "right." Once the roots are established, though, the giant bamboo can grow several feet per day.

PREFACE

When I finally published *Dear Fellow Spender* in 2023, it was during a serious chapter of personal exploration. The husband and kids I'd always wanted had not yet materialized, despite lots of dating and some close calls. You could say that I was take a good long hard look at what I wanted my life to look like if it continued to not include a family of my own.

Over the preceding several years, I'd written multiple drafts of a book about my own financial transformation. I had learnings and "ah ha" moments to share around getting out of debt, discovering budget as a *happy* thing, saving seriously, and trusting myself with money. The book was mostly finished and was oh so safely stored on my Google Drive—where it could help exactly no one. The leaps I'd taken in the preceding months finally propelled me to polish it up and share it with the world.

Those leaps included leaving a cushy corporate job to focus on my financial coaching business, Moso Money, and do some of that personal exploration I mentioned. At that point, I thought the audience I could most help in my business and with my book was women. There is some truth in saying that, for us women, money can be an emotional experience. Even though I'd coached men and very much enjoyed it, it felt easier to write for those I'd primarily talked with—women who'd never enjoyed managing money before. I wanted to help them discover how they too could afford a comfortable, guilt-free-spending sort of life.

But as I traveled Europe and the United States for two years, coaching, writing, and talking with loads of strangers, I realized a few important things.

First, I didn't want to be just a writer or coach for women or solo women. Most of us—male or female, married or currently solo—want to live meaningful lives, and I want to talk with and write for anyone who wants that same thing. Plus, we're not all that different, and have way more in common than we don't.

Secondly, as I chose to let go of the perceived certainty of a paycheck and work on my own things, I have come to appreciate even more the value of trusting yourself with money. The amount of money we have or make is not in our direct or lasting control, but supportive habits make the most of whatever money we *do* have.

Thirdly, it's profoundly true that money is only a piece of a wealthy life, and that more *living* is what I care most about, for myself and for others. I came to care much less about comfort, and way more about personal growth.

These days, I rarely write specifically about money. Instead, I write sometimes humorous and occasionally insightful things about life and travel and people and embracing uncertainty. I've recently published my second book, *Dear Fellow Dreamer: Waking Up, Taking Chances, and Creating A Life of Your Own.* And the coaching work I do with individuals centers even more on the principled, dream-filled life you want to create, and how to create more organization and personal autonomy to support those goals.

This book remains mostly as written those years ago, despite there being things the perfectionist in me would love to revise. In a revised edition, I'd be less hard on myself, for one. I'd add even more encouragement for you to be compassionate with yourself and your financial past and present. That said, I'm letting it stand largely as the 2023 version of Emily published it. The main change is that I've softened language that made male readers wonder if this book was for them. It absolutely is. *Spender*—our nickname for this book—is for anyone who knows financial stress, doesn't like it, and wants to spend their money and life in more peaceful and meaningful ways.

Emily Burnett

2025

INTRODUCTION

S he won $10.5 million in 2004. Nine years later, it was entirely gone, and she was commuting—by bus—to a part-time job.

Another woman who won $3.9 million, and then another $1.4 million in 1985, was broke and living in a trailer park by the year 2000.

A third winner won $1.3 million in 1994, and nine years later it was all gone. Not only was it gone, she was also $154,000 in debt.

Another winner won $18 million in 1993. Eight years later she was filing for bankruptcy for debts totaling $2.5 million and had less than $700 in her accounts.[1] The list could go on and on. The list, that is, of lottery winners who prove two universal truths. One, that life and unexpected events—good and bad—can happen to all of us, and two, that more money may not be the answer to your problems.

Not at first, at least.

Human resource directors, attorneys, VPs, stay-at-home parents, entrepreneurs, therapists, nurses, grad students, single people, divorced people, podcasters, physicians—basically, all kinds of people, in all kinds of life stages. These are just some of the types of people with whom I've had financial conversations.

And nearly every one of them is positive that more money is going to solve any money problem and many of their life problems. The most helpful news I love to share is that—barring very few exceptions—you don't need more money to change your money life. And in fact, until you fix your *approach* to money management and start to take care of what you have, more money may only magnify your financial stress.

Despite your feelings about cold, hard cash, money management isn't hard. Sure, there are complicated concepts and strategies and verbiage, but at its core, money just involves simple math. If you can add, subtract, multiply, and divide, you are amply qualified to manage your money. If you figured out how to acquire this book, I feel safe assuming you can perform basic math, and this bodes very well for your financial future.

Where it gets complicated is at the feelings level. Feelings take something very factual, and turn it into a combination of a rollercoaster and the Teacup ride at Disneyland that makes everyone over the age of seven sick.

This book is written from a non-frugal woman to others who similarly don't feel frugal. And it is written with the intent to convince you to take the reins of your monthly money, starting with proactive cash-flow planning.

> Budgeting— the active cycle of organizing your money and planning your spending—is a profound gift you can give not only your future life, but your life *right now*.

Doing so pays dividends now and in the future. It helps you:

- Make peace with all the feelings you currently have about money and your relationship with it.

- Face the facts of your current and any future situation.

- Enjoy your spending (or choice to not spend) more.

- Choose an empowered path forward.

Sound like things you can get on board with? So far, so good, then.

This book is dedicated to anyone who is stressed about money. It starts by setting the stage for the conversation about money management, budgeting, and dreaming big that we are about to have. Then, we delve into seven life-changing benefits of proactive money management. The final third of the book shows you what it can look like.

Why dedicate so many words to selling you on positive money management and budgeting before we dive into the actual implementation? Well, there are legitimate reasons why you haven't wanted to do it and it would be downright dismissive to tell you that it should be easy and jump right into, "Here's how you manage your money." You've had enough of that kind of messaging; it's time for a more compassionate, relatable approach.

If you stick with me and are convinced that budgeting— proactively managing your money—is something you want to do, *the doing* becomes the easy part. And to set you up for success, you get step-by-step instructions for actually budgeting in a way you can love.

I can't sell you motivation or give you mine, but what I can do is try to highlight for you—from the viewpoint of someone who's been a financial mess and remains a spender—all the benefits of proactively managing your money. I suspect you'll find as I have that there are only upsides to having a handle on money. This book is written from friend to friend, and does not address the complexities of relationship dynamics. It is written to encourage every reader to be active in what they can control, to be a fully contributing adult in household money management. Regardless of your life situation, you are a grown-up with a very cool future to take into consideration, and being as proactive as possible with your money sets you up to create a really good life.

This is not a book about "living frugally forever" or "10 ways to live on the cheap." I don't care for the word "frugal" and certainly don't live a frugal life myself. Intentional, yes. Frugal, no. The main reason I avoided honest budgeting for so long was that I thought it would necessitate frugal living. This to me implied a lifetime prohibition on anything fun or nice. It sounded boring and restrictive. And ew, who wants that?

You may naturally identify as "frugal," and this book can still be for you! But this book is primarily written for the spenders, the budget-resisters, the ones who think they can't do it or don't want to do it.

This book could be called so many things: *In Defense of Budgeting*, or *Budgeting That Doesn't Ruin Your Life*, or *An Attempt to Reframe Budgeting For Those who Loathe the Word as Much as I Used To*. Especially the latter wouldn't work very well on a book cover, hence the current title.

Because "budgeting" can be sensitive territory for many of us, let me clarify my use of the word. For the purposes of this book, when I talk about budgeting or having a plan, I am solely referring to the process of proactively planning your spending in accordance with your plans and priorities instead of reacting to everything coming at you.

These milestones are a main part of the reason you budget in the first place—you are organizing your money to take care of the necessities and wants of life and to make tangible progress toward your goals. "Budget" does not imply restriction or deprivation or misery. If I've said it once, I'll say it twice, since budgeting as a word and as a practice has gotten rather maligned.

What I am writing about is the benefits of getting on a plan. We're talking about an intentional, proactive spending plan that matches the plans you have for your life.

Like, what do you want to do in your lifetime? What do you want to learn, contribute, donate to, experience, enjoy? Do you want to travel, live in a yurt in the Himalayas for a year, retire in ease at 50? Build an orphanage in Africa, drive an Audi?

I don't know what you plan for your life to be. But when you get clear on what you want to do/be/have/accomplish, you have given yourself a really big reason to think differently about your money.

If the benefits of budgeting were more widely understood, everyone would do it. The most widely-accepted benefit of budgeting is that you'll have more money, but that alone doesn't seem to be motivating for the 55% of people who don't budget.[2] There are so many benefits to budgeting, that if more widely known, would make *doing* it a no-brainer. And that is the point of this book.

I feel like shouting this message from the rooftops to others. To people with big plans for their life: buying their first house, or a house on their own; starting a business; learning that new skill; taking a year to provide humanitarian relief. Plans they don't think they'll ever achieve because they have to stay in their self-imposed financial prison. People who have given up hope that things can be different.

This book is written to show those in a close relationship with debt that there is a different way. Debt has most likely not been your friend. With ready access to financing—it was news to me that people finance *furniture*!—it has been way too easy to put your potential and your plans in prison.

Or at the very least, shackle them. I chased many a dream with debt and then, because I didn't have a plan for paying off that debt, had to drag it along with me into my next goal and venture. Talk about buzzkill.

It may seem like an exaggeration to claim financial freedom is truly the gateway to other kinds of freedom, but I know it's not. I'm not talking about having millions in the bank and never having to work again. I'm talking about living on less than you make, planning your spending (budgeting), having money in savings, and low or no debt. This combination allows you loads more options in life than when you have no financial breathing room and really unhelpful habits.

Money is the basic currency for anything you want to improve, have or do in this life—relationships, businesses, bucket list items, generosity. Making a plan for it, and getting the roots of money right by budgeting, allows for growth in all these other areas.

When I bring up money, especially budgeting (and I bring it up a lot), the response I get more than any other is a shoulder shrug, a look of guilt, and something to the effect of, "I really should do that." This defeated response makes me want to gently grab the responder by the shoulders, give them a friendly shake and tell them, "No! This is not a chore to feel awful about! This is something amazing you can want to do!"

Budgeting with a purpose is the best thing I ever did for myself and my life, and it will be for you, too.

And I love what I'm building on this foundation. Helping others find the same joy and freedom I found by making a plan for my money instead of letting it spend itself is something I'm deeply passionate about. Hence this book, written in three parts.

Part One is where I earn my street cred with you and set the stage for the rest of the conversation we're going to have. I fully understand unhappy money management and had to learn that budgeting and being a spender were not mutually exclusive. My knowledge is not merely theoretical.

Oh heavens no. I learned it through making all kinds of mistakes. Credit card debt? Check. Cannot even count how many credit cards I've had over my lifetime. Student loans? Yes, which is a little sad considering my education was incredibly affordable for an institution of its caliber. Car loans? Check, check. There was also a personal loan along the way, along with countless overdraft fees, pinching pennies after overspending, and sleepless nights. I made all the mistakes, and still pulled through okay because of what I finally learned about money.

Part Two includes seven life-changing benefits of proactive money management and is written for the reluctant budgeters like myself—the ones who are afraid of it ruining their life. It is written for the dreamers who have big plans for life and grand things to accomplish, but have been mired in money mediocrity. It is dedicated to *why* everyone should want to budget.

If you get the roots of *anything* right, growth is infinitely more possible and uncapped. But sometimes we all need to be sold on the benefits. With these seven benefits of budgeting, I'm helping you sell yourself on why you want to get on a plan. A plan that you make for yourself, a plan that your potential asks of you, and a plan that reciprocally makes your potential possible.

Part Three is devoted to showing you *how* to organize your money—budget—to make these dreams possible. To make life less complicated and stressful. To take care of what you have so you are well-prepared to receive more.

You are smart. You will figure budgeting out once you see how much sense it can make and realize what's at stake if you don't. And more importantly, you will stick with it after seeing these benefits realized in your life.

In short, this book is meant to persuade you—yes, you— that today is the day to do money and life differently, then show you how. You have contributions to make to the world only you can make that are not being realized. By getting your money roots right, you can stop spending your best energies fighting financial fires and trying to make ends meet.

You may be tempted to skip ahead to Part Three. Don't. We've got work to do on your motivation first, even if you think you're ready.

Ready to dive in? Let's get to it.

PART 1: THE BACKGROUND

Part 1 of the book is all about setting the stage for the money and "proactive money management" conversation we're about to have. Yes, we could dive right into the life-changing benefits of taking care of the money you already have, or how you do that, but it's critical that you first see just how stuck I was, how I got there, and more importantly how I found my way forward.

I've said many times that if I can do this whole money transformation thing, so can anyone. Money is such an emotional experience, and it's important to me that you know that I "get" the feelings around it. I've also talked with hundreds of people about money and have seen clearly what does and does not work when it comes to money and life changes. Some of those stories are woven throughout.

In Part 2, we talk about the life-changing benefits of proactive money management (or taking care of your money in the way I teach). And then in Part 3, I walk you through the process that finally worked for me. By then, I hope you'll be excited and beyond ready to begin your own money transformation so you can stop living small. But I'm getting ahead of myself. We've got a stage to set, so let's do that without further ado.

Chapter 1

THE "MADE IT" MOMENT

My largely magical childhood included dreams of a club-house I was going to build with my little brother. We were a preteen and a young teenager as we saved our hard-earned money for said clubhouse. Mowing lawns, working for Dad at the shop, doing extra chores around the house, babysitting, and collecting insects for biological weed control. Yes, I collected bugs and made incredible money at one of the world's least glamorous jobs.

My brother and I had planned out our lumber needs and costs, sketched our design and clubhouse features time and time again, and fantasized about how cool it would be to have our very own place. But young teenage life happened and this spender squandered her part of the money on... literally nothing that lasted. I still feel bad, both that I missed out on actually building a structure with my own two hands, but more so that I abandoned the dream and what would have been a great memory with my brother.

Fast forward a few, oh, 23 years.

It was a rainy night and my sister-in-law was in town visiting. The wife of said brother, as it happens. We'd just been out to dinner and were picking up some baked goods on the way home. Trying out a new bakery, we got to chatting with the girl behind the counter. By the time she rang up my purchase (a decadent gluten-free, vegan, peanut butter fudge brownie bar even though I'm not gluten sensitive or vegan) we had a nice rapport going.

She told me my total, I gave her my debit card, and she asked if I would like a receipt. I responded with, "Oh, that's all right, I'll just enter it in my budgeting app," and I pulled out my phone to do so.

Here's where the story gets interesting. I exaggerate, but I bet you'll keep reading anyway. No response was necessary since I had pulled out my phone and was beginning to enter my purchase when she said something to the effect of, "I need to do that." Not everyone would see that as an open door but when you now love budgeting like I do, it's as if she flung the barn door open wide and said, "Come on in!" This led to a minutes-long conversation about the budgeting app I use, my business as a money coach, and spending and money habits in general. Lest you think I was monologuing about budgeting, it was most definitely a true conversation. Proof: She asked for and wrote down the name of my blog on a scrap of receipt.

I wonder where my bakery friend is today. But no matter where she is, I hope she is still involved in making such fabulous treats and, hopefully, budgeting. Similar renditions of this encounter have been repeated countless times.

TYPICAL RESPONSES

When I tell people I'm a money coach and that budgeting changed my life, I typically get one of three responses.

Response 1

A number of people respond with, "I should do that." They say this with a defeated tone and slumped shoulders, as if they just told me they need to get a root canal or give up sugar. Levels of guilt or reluctance vary, but many responses include the words "should" or "need." Or their spouse wants them to be more invested in their money management or to get on board with budgeting.

Within this group, there are many who feel defeated at the mere mention of all the money words, like "budget" and "savings." But they don't say anything. They just wallow in self-loathing, feeling anxious and embarrassed.

As someone who spent years and almost multiple decades in budget denial and avoidance, I get it. Words like "frugal," "cheap," and "budget" elicited an almost visceral reaction in me. They evoked complicated feelings of guilt, shame, and rebellion. Honestly, some of those words still do—especially that rebellion one. In my past, I tried to avoid any conversation about them. It's no wonder why, when the mental image my brain painted was a dismal picture of a no-fun-ever, bleak existence eating store brand Raisin Bran purchased on bulk discount with powdered milk (it's cheaper). No thanks! There was no way I wanted to voluntarily sign myself up for such a life!

For people I know in real life in this category, they often follow up privately with me. It's like the dirty laundry you don't talk about until it's brought up, but once it's out there, it is such a relief to share with someone else.

When I share that I paid off $50,000 in debt and used to twitch at the mere mention of "budgeting," the taboo subject becomes so much more approachable. This has led to some fabulous talks, broken-budget rants, and encouragement sessions over text, Zoom, telephone, and in person as a coach, friend, and family member.

Response 2

Another group of people are those eager to tell me budgeting doesn't work. Or that they'd only do it if it was easy, and if it's not easy, quick, or painless, it's not for them. That they don't have time. They launch into what they dislike about financial experts or popular apps.

The response is almost one of defiance. Like, "I don't need to change anything. I am in charge of this ship (nevermind that it's a mess). I don't need a new system or tool or approach, I just need more money, and I'm working on attracting more money to me with positive thinking or living in abundance." I still love these people! I've just learned that their moment of change has not quite arrived. That, for a multitude of reasons, they are not ready to change. If you find yourself in this category, please keep reading! Because this book is very much for you, too, with lots of hope that I can help you start to entertain different possibilities for your money and your life.

Response 3

And then there's another category of people. Of people who really are doing it! And feel peaceful about money. No guilt or shame or defense. Those conversations are usually a celebration of the results we love getting.

> And that's the whole point of budgeting—to have more peace and enjoy sweet financial *results*.

However, in my experience, and statistically speaking, that latter category is the minority. Even those making six-figure or more income often do not feel peaceful or settled about their money or choices with it. A CNBC article reports that in early 2022, 64% of U.S. households were living paycheck to paycheck.[3] That's a lot of stress and uncertainty for a lot of people.

Even those in more comfortable circumstances have a tenuous relationship with debt, buy lots of luxuries, never really know what they can truly afford, and are not firmly in control of planning their monthly money. They don't have a compelling reason to organize their money differently, except to maintain an ever encroaching lifestyle or keep up with inflation.

Large incomes often lead to bigger purchases, decisions, and sense of aimlessness and may not always be the blessing they superficially seem to be.

So, which bucket are you in? How do you respond to questions or conversations about money? Defeated and willing to talk about it, or privately embarrassed Resistant/excuse-laden Peaceful Even if you're in one of the first two groups, there is loads of hope for you. I shared the stories at the beginning of this chapter to illustrate just how possible it is for a spender to become a happy budgeter.

To have switched from the person squandering cash to talking about the benefits of money management with anyone who will listen, is nothing short of profound. Basically, if I can do it, so can you.

Chapter 2

THE TURNING POINT

So where did I start? I was broke, stuck, and ashamed. I'd received a raise at work a few months earlier—a raise which, when delivered made me think, "I'm rich! I can afford anything I want now!" It was a 68% increase over my salary at a previous job just one year earlier, a 13% increase from my starting salary at that current job, and I was ecstatic.

Trips to Thailand and Iceland, barre studio memberships, organic produce, a personal dating coach, over-the-top gifts for family and friends...I could do it all now! Conjure in your mind an image of someone throwing money around with reckless abandon, and that's how I felt.

But not so fast.

MY SPENDING DECISIONS

You see, over the previous sixteen years I had accumulated a nice, ahem, portfolio. Too bad that "portfolio" was composed of debt and poor spending habits. The most prominent spending habit was one of putting things on credit cards at the slight thought that the situation with my real money was getting a little tight, or when I ran out of real money. It wasn't as if I was literally or figuratively flushing my money down the toilet: I had not been outside the country since 2003 (Brazil), I hadn't purchased a time-share, I had not purchased expensive memberships or bought land in Montana or eaten at all the best restaurants in town. Basically, there were dumber, more irresponsible things I could have done with my money.

What I did instead is waste my money a few dollars here, and $100 there. Another $20 here, and $600 there on a not-planned-for vacation with friends. It's hard to remember all the perpetual overspending on groceries and dining out at the many restaurants and the quick trips here and there and getting cash back at the grocery store and having no clue where that cash went. All these instances of overspending or unplanned-for spending ranged from modest to glamorous, and led to tens of thousands of dollars in debt.

Note: This was not the entirety of my life-time debt "accomplishment." I figure my total debt "experience" (like a theme park thrill ride but significantly less fun) to be over $100K. A car accident settlement allowed me to pay off medical debt, the replacement car

I'd bought with debt, and some consumer debt. But I hadn't yet learned how to proactively manage my money, and it was easy to slip back into old patterns.

Anyway, back to my second debt peak of $50,000. That amount of debt meant that something like $1,100 of my income every single month was spoken for. $1,100 of my hard-earned income every single month was paying for things that had occurred in my past and, for the most part, were not blessing my present or future.

My monthly debt payments went to a car loan, student loans still kicking around from college, and multiple credit cards. I'd used the latter to pay for living expenses during a web development bootcamp in the Bay Area and to fund business ideas which never launched. I essentially chased my dreams with credit cards and no plan for repayment aside from striking it big. Picture a prospector hoping to strike the mother lode, and welcome to my 20's.

Note: Retooling my career and entering tech is part of what was responsible for a significant increase in my salary and earning potential, so I have no regrets about doing it. In hindsight, I might just have approached it differently.

Back to the pay-raise. The raise I'd received translated to a nice bump in my paychecks, but I quickly adjusted to the increase as I unintentionally increased my lifestyle to match the higher salary. A conscious yet lax effort to actually budget over the previous five months had heightened my awareness about my spending habits, but given my now-higher income, I felt like I could certainly afford to spend more in every category.

Except that I still had tens of thousands of dollars worth of debt hanging over my head. It was like the perpetual gray cloud in an otherwise gorgeous blue sky. It felt like a fetter around my ankle, just a "little something" that went everywhere with me: vacations, church, dates, shopping, hiking, family time, hanging out with friends.

And it felt like it would be with me forever since, even though I now made good money and faithfully paid my monthly payments, I was making only minimal progress on getting rid of the debt. I was sure I would be a grandmother still paying on the student loans it was ridiculous I had acquired in the first place.

THE TURNING POINT

But something changed. Well, a couple things changed. I had been dating a guy who owned his own home, had no debt that I was aware of or that he admitted, had a job he loved, and had the ability to play a lot with pretty cool toys—rock climbing gear, mountain bikes, road bikes, motorcycles, etc. In comparing myself financially to him, I always came up short. That is, until my sister pointed out that he was 5 years ahead of me in life and asked how long it would take me to pay off my debt.

What a question! Being in debt forever felt like a fact. And I had therefore never made a plan around my debt payoff. It goes to show that we can get acclimated to situations, even miserable and stressful ones. Rational problem-solving goes out the window until something happens to interrupt our narrative of what is or isn't possible.

This question gave me pause, and introduced a new possibility that perhaps I could pay off my debt. And perhaps within the next five years. This novel thought was accompanied with a glimmer of hope. To surface a plan, I invited my sister over for a raw look at my numbers. A sisters' date, if you will. Agenda item: review my finances. Doesn't that sound like an absolute party?!

The outcome of that conversation was the exhilarating realization that I could be debt-free in 3.5 years. And still live well, buy gifts, and take vacations during the payoff. Hallelujah! It felt like I'd been serving a life sentence and found out I would actually be released in just 3.5 years. Everything was mapped out—the now-positive difference between my income and my realistic spending, which debt I was paying off first and by what date, which debt was next, and so on.

Now that my budget and my money life had a purpose and had been exposed to the light of day, I finally, for the first time in my life, made rapid progress. My debt-payoff goal of 42 months turned into 20 months, and in February 2017 I paid off my last debt—my car.

THE RESULTS

For the first time in several years, I had not a payment in the world. The $1,150 that had basically been garnished from my wages due to the monthly payments I had signed myself up for, was mine, all gloriously mine. It was as if I had, overnight, received an awesome raise.

Having more money was awesome. Equally awesome was the fact that I was no longer obligated to pay so much money every month. My monthly expenses decreased by the $1,150 I no longer had to pay toward debt, which made me feel rich with options. If I'd wanted to quit my salaried job and work at a pie shop for much less than my current salary, I could do that. If I wanted to travel to Europe for a month, I wasn't on the hook for any debt payments while gone. It was a wonderful and novel feeling.

HOW I TURNED THE SHIP AROUND

I attribute my financial turnaround to three critical changes: getting very real with my current situation, focusing on one financial priority at a time, and using a system that kept it all organized. Let's have a little chat about those three critical things, shall we?

Change 1

In that absolute party of a conversation with my sister, I surfaced all of my spending and debts. Not what I wished they were, or was willing to admit to, but what they really were. All the things I pretended I didn't do, like eat out, buy clothes, get my hair done, buy make-up, take vacations. I also got as real as possible about how much all the more practical parts of life cost, including the annual expenses amortized into monthly amounts.

Change 2

Instead of trying to do all the good and responsible things at once, I focused on one thing at a time. Previously, I'd tried to build my savings, invest in retirement, and pay down multiple debts at one time. Can you guess how well that went?

Anyway, at this crucial juncture, I picked one thing to do. That first thing was to save $1,000 to function as my new buffer. And it served to get me out of the habit of turning to the credit card when things felt tight. Because of what I implemented in the other two changes, this emergency buffer was finally able to serve as an actual emergency fund—hallelujah. With this in place, I picked one debt—my smallest—to pay off as quickly as possible while making minimum payments on all the other debts. When that debt was paid off, the money I'd been throwing at it went toward Debt #2. Anytime I had a setback or had to use my emergency fund for something that was truly unexpected and couldn't be covered from elsewhere in my budget, I paused this process and rebuilt my savings. Then, back to the debt.

Change 3

And then I started budgeting in earnest. The budget was just how I kept everything organized and where I planned my real dollars. Oh sure, I'd budgeted before. Rather, I'd "budgeted" before. Spreadsheets, apps, cash envelopes, spending freezes. They'd work for a few months or until something happened to rock my precariously organized situation.

The tool I started using at this point just clicked. It refuted my previous conceptions of a budget as something restrictive and depriving. That tool was—and remains—an integral part of my bigger financial management system. It was just the right vehicle to help me get where I wanted to go.

But just like any vehicle, it was no good on its own. It simply gave me a place to organize all the things I'd been trying to juggle. No more trying to keep track of my plans and expenses in my head or on spreadsheets, scribbles on paper, and multiple savings accounts—now I had a single place to organize everything and interact with my plans.

It operates as a zero-based budget, which means you give every dollar of your money a purpose, but unlike other apps, you only do this with the money you actually have. Some other apps allow you to budget the money you are going to get that month and track against that. If that has worked for you, great. But if, like me, you have found that a hypothetical spreadsheet or tool alone cannot keep up with a busy life, you will love how well this method works. Spreadsheets can be a critical management tool for forecasting your anticipated money and seeing how you plan to spend your next future paychecks. My money management process happily includes a spreadsheet, but reframing budgeting as something that you do with real, present money makes a critical difference.

LIFE AFTER DEBT

So, what did life look like right after becoming debt-free? Did I jet off on a trip to Thailand, buy a place in Iceland (is that actually even possible for a US citizen?), start working out at the fancy gym with a personal trainer, eat only organic produce, and hire a personal dating coach named Chad?

No. I didn't do any of those things, at least not right away, and I have yet to hire a personal dating coach named Chad or any other name. You see, even though my goal had been to pay off my debt, the habits I developed along the way changed me. My relationship with money and with spending and with life priorities was changed. Thailand, Iceland, organic eggplant, luxury gyms and Chad could all be in my future—but only if they fit into the greater plan and purpose I now had for my money and my life.

In the recent years, I have been to Belize, Ireland, Germany, and several countries in southern Europe; bolstered my "Clothing and Luxuries" budget category; picked up some new outdoor hobbies (looking at you, e-MTB and fly fishing); traveled a lot in the United States; enjoyed good meals; taken myself on annual personal goal retreats; been more generous with others; bought a home; built a comfortable emergency fund; paid cash for personal development and business courses; and so much more.

The changes that falling in love with this type of financial management—allocating money in accordance with my priorities and plan—have made in my life are immeasurable. I don't share the list of things purchased or done since becoming debt-free to gloat. Not at all.

I share it as part of reframing budgeting for those who, like me for so long, think that you only budget when you're poor, and that there's no room in a budget for so much fun stuff. The opposite has been and is true for me, my clients, and anyone who embraces the above simple principles, especially a budget that keeps everything organized and on track. Are you beginning to understand why budgeting has become my favorite thing to talk about and help others with?

Chapter 3

WHY WE AVOID OUR MONEY

M indy didn't budget because they had plenty of money. She was the household money manager for a family of six and did a great job of keeping all the bills paid. Their investment goals were being met with their work with a financial planner.

They afforded all the trips and clothes and kids' lessons they wanted, and still lived comfortably within their income. Why wasn't she budgeting? Yes, she was busy and didn't "need to" in the same way that Lindsay did. But the frank reason for not budgeting was that she'd feel more guilty about their lavish lifestyle. Lindsay is a single woman who doesn't actively budget because she is terrified of what she will find. She uses credit cards to keep her lifestyle afloat and doesn't want anyone to know how strapped she is. She doesn't want to come face to face with

her situation, fearing that when she does, she will have to stop
spending money on the things she loves buying and having.

How many U.S. households create a monthly budget? According to CreditDonkey, just 32%.[4] And in a survey by credit.com,
some of the reasons why people avoid budgeting are highlighted:

- 24% of respondents don't think they'll stick to it.

- 10% of respondents don't feel like making one.

- 15% of respondents don't want to feel restricted by a
  budget.

- 10% of respondents don't know how to get started.

- 12% of respondents are afraid to even check their bank
  account.[5]

I would also add that budgeting has been seriously slandered. If
budgeting was a person, its reputation would be not very fun,
punishing, and super boring. If you're reading this book, I would
guess this has been your opinion. It certainly was mine for years,
as you now know.

> Budgeting seemed like a restrictive authority figure instead of
> the wind in my sails. I'm guessing you can relate.

In my work as a financial coach, and in conversations with dozens
of others, here are common attitudes I come across.

- Budgeting means deprivation, so no thanks.

- I've tried it and it doesn't work.

- Money management can't require any effort from me.

- Only poor people budget, and I'm not poor—therefore I don't need one.

- I'm not smart enough.

- I'm too smart.

- It's confusing or hard.

- I don't have any extra money to budget.

- We're in the middle of a month or year; I'll start next month/year.

- I'm afraid of my/our numbers. It's easier not to know.

- A budget means I can't buy the things I want, so I'm going to buy all the things and then start.

Several years ago, a cousin recommended a personal finance book. It was chock-full of sound, timeless, and practical financial advice. Things like: live on less than you make, don't get into debt/pay it off, pay cash for stuff, save a portion of everything you make, use a budget. You know, good stuff.

I read it, could see the value in all those ideas...then put it away and continued to spend like I made the big bucks and was debt-free. Neither was true. But I remember thinking explicitly: "I'll come back to this book when I'm debt-free and making more money." To be honest, I felt guilty. For someone who doesn't like to be told what to do and felt ashamed of my spending and debt, I wanted to just bury my head in the sand.

Basically, I can relate to most if not all of the attitudes above. Now that I've been on both sides of the fence, one attitude deserves a special award for doing the best job of keeping people stuck. That is the excuse of "I've tried budgeting, and it doesn't work." First, it assumes that all approaches to budgeting are equal (they're not), that because you've tried one system, you've tried them all (you haven't), or that you gave it everything you have (did you, really?) Second, it closes you off to trying anything or considering any new information or a different approach.

Unlike learned helplessness in which an animal learns that, no matter what they try, they are powerless to change their circumstance, most people making this excuse have not sincerely embraced a proactive approach to money management. But because they don't acknowledge that, they remain resistant to anything that might actually help them or firmly opposed to seriously trying something that they half-heartedly tried previously.

A conversation with one prospective client comes to mind. Jacki spent most of our initial call telling me why none of the suggestions we were discussing would work for her. She had a comeback for everything, and an excuse for why to not even consider my suggestions or recommendations. I recognize now, with a lot more coaching experience, that she was in what's known as the pre-contemplation stage of change and truly was not ready to make any changes.[6]

A life-changing budgeting system can never be launched from a position of skepticism. Why? At the mere whisper of friction (a question, a balance you don't understand, overspending), your doubts are confirmed: "Ah ha! I knew this wouldn't work!" And you go back to your familiar routines of not budgeting and being comfortable with the perpetual stress.

I suppose it's possible you have actually tried all the approaches, given each of them a legit amount of effort, and still not succeeded. But once you get honest with yourself, you might realize like I did that you have just dabbled in various budgeting systems. I gave budgeting 25% effort and expected 100% results, then blamed the system for not bringing me amazing results.

"THIS IS SOUNDING LIKE ME..."

If anything in this section describes you, please don't stop reading! I spent a lot of time in this category myself, and I say all of this with no judgment. Nothing about it is intended to make you feel lame or make you defensive, only to facilitate a wake-up call much sooner than I had mine.

Imagine a hypothetical conversation about money between the two of us. How do you think you would respond?

1. "My homemade spreadsheet system is superior to anything else out there. Even if my results aren't great there is nothing else worth trying."

2. "I need to keep doing/affording all the things. Our/my kids are only young once and I want to give them fun things/experiences even if it means continuing our debt spiral." Or: "I deserve all the fun things and experiences I afford for myself, whether I can afford them or not."

3. "I want to be a good steward of the abundance in my life, but the budgeting system can't involve much effort from me at all. If it takes more than a few minutes a month, it's just not going to work for me."

4. "My plan is just not to spend money; I don't need a budget. They're great for other people, though."

5. "I'm ready."

You may relate to Responses A-D listed above, but you're reaching or have reached a point where you're ready to be done with them. Done with all the confusion and constant juggling of amounts between accounts. Done with all the "emergencies" that pop up to surprise you. Done with never making progress on your goals. Done with acquiring debt with no plan to pay it off.

It's a magical spot to arrive at— being ready for something different. Enough is enough.

Here are the things that indicate readiness to me: You listen to understand, not to refute or defend. "Budgeting" is not on trial. In fact, nothing and no one is on trial.

You are willing to look at and share all your spending and debt amounts. No more hiding behind vague numbers that you don't want anyone to see. You're done being ashamed, and ready to get to work.

You are willing to look at and accept your present situation. If you are spending more than you make, you are totally okay knowing that and making some different decisions to change that. You are done not knowing.

You are willing to learn a new system, recognizing it just might deliver results better than the system you've been using that isn't working. "Not working" means you deal with cycles of:

- Continually accumulated more debt

- Yo-yo'ing with debt

- Dealing with frequent expense surprises

- A near-constant feeling of stress about money and affording your life

- Living paycheck-to-paycheck

- Doing all the good things but making no appreciable headway on goals like debt-payoff, saving, investing.

Let's talk about Driver's Education for a second. With each passing year, I appreciate more the early-morning risk my teacher took by riding in a car driven on snowy Montana roads by clueless teenagers. Anyway, you know how it's easy to pass judgment on your student driver friend from the backseat, or think you know all the answers? Then Mr. Watkins says, "Ok, Burnett. Your turn." Suddenly, you can't remember things like how much room you need to leave between you and the vehicle in front of you at a stoplight and who yields to who at stop signs. Only then do you start asking questions, realizing you have very little incentive to hide what you don't remember, and a lot of incentive—safety, passing the class, and a lifetime of driving opportunity—to ask questions.

In like manner, those who I've seen succeed with money are willing to finally pour their effort and energy into moving *forward*. They don't have anything to defend. They ask questions, realizing that there is no time like now to get answers. They are curious and make fewer and fewer excuses. They no longer view mistakes as proof that budgeting doesn't work or that money is hard or that they are dumb, and they simply clean up any small messes along the way, learn stuff, and keep moving forward.

Could this be you? Even if you're not entirely convinced, please keep reading! You made it this far, which says a lot about you. You want something different; you're just still coming around.

This book could be—and if I have anything to do with it, it will be—your moment where you catch the vision of why basic money stewardship matters so much, why it's so awesome, and how you do it in a way that doesn't ruin your life.

Chapter 4

BUDGETING THAT WORKS

BUDGETING AS MOST PEOPLE DO IT

Traditional budgeting is what nearly every person is presently doing. Well, every person who earns income, pays their bills, and doesn't want to go to collections or overdraft their accounts. You know, the sort of person likely reading this book. I mention this to increase your openness to budgeting, by helping you see that you're technically already doing a form of it.

Eventually every reasonably responsible person on the planet has to live within the limits of their income and has to do at least some mental organization to do so. Whether you are formally budgeting or not, you literally have to do some version of it in order to meet your expenses and pay for luxuries and wants.

That's budgeting at its highest level, and it should be comforting that you are already doing that.

In a little more detail, here is what traditional budgeting looks like:

1. You make X amount of money.

2. Your bills/monthly spending on necessities total Y.

3. You *should* have X-Y = Z left over for savings and wants.

4. You mentally allocate how much you are putting toward flexible spending categories like Groceries. Bonus effort points for entering that spending into a spreadsheet or a budgeting app.

5. Keep an eye on your Checking account balance to see how much money you have left. If you have a lot, you can buy things.

6. The checking account gets alarmingly low when you pay the annual Amazon Prime membership fee *and* semi-annual insurance premium that you forgot were happening this month.

7. You panic, mentally flog yourself, transfer in money from savings, and resolve to be better/more disciplined/ frugal next month.

This form of mental-gymnastics-budgeting can be like a bad dance between reactive behavior, good intentions, and frustration at overspending. The question to ask yourself is: "Is what I'm doing *working* for me?" How well is your system covering your wants and needs and goals?

The same thing happens on a credit card, with more sinister consequences since you can spend up to the available credit limit. Can you relate to a friend of mine who cringes each month she opens her credit card statement, curious to see how much she spent? Research shows that people spend more—significantly more—on a credit card than when they have to pay immediately with real money.

In a study by two professors at Massachusetts Institute of Technology, participants who had to pay with a credit card were willing to spend *twice* as much for last-minute NBA tickets than participants who had to pay cash.[7] A similar study by the company Dun & Bradstreet found that people spend 12% to 18% more when they use a credit card than when they use cash (real money).

I'm not trying to ruin your beautiful relationships with "significant others" like Chase, Visa, and Mastercard. I just am personally not a fan of using credit cards unless you are committed to planning your spending and living within your income.

Credit cards did me no favors over my 15 years of intimate use and enabled my poor planning for too long. However, it is entirely possible to have a healthy relationship with credit cards if you pair their use with a real, living budget. More on this later!

ZERO-BASED BUDGETING

Alternatively, a zero-based budget works only with the money you have right now. And it will change your life.

I didn't invent zero-based budgeting. I am also not the only person in the world who knows how amazing it is. It's not as if I'm selling you on a special oil that, if rubbed on your left elbow every Tuesday, will cure all your ailments.

Put simply, zero-based budgeting means giving a purpose to each dollar you receive until you have no more dollars. It's budgeting that you do whenever you get money, not something you do hypothetically or only on the first of the month. And it's all about allocating actual dollars for what you need and want to cover until you get more money.

A zero-based budget partners very well with a spreadsheet where you've planned for several months down the road. The hypothetical plan gives you the long-view many people consider to be budgeting. But true budgeting refers to actually allocating all of your current money to specific purposes and is not a monthly event.

Happy budgeting is more of an ongoing conversation between you, your money, and your wants, needs and priorities.

You plan your immediate spending with current money only,
influenced by your knowledge of what your money needs to
cover before you get more, then adjust as needed.

Zero-based budgeting can be further described with a practical
example. You may be familiar with the "envelope system" popu-
larized by the likes of Dave Ramsey, but in case not, please allow
me to explain it briefly.

Let's say on payday you get $2,700. You have an envelope or a
cubby for every expense category in your life, very much including the fun stuff. You start putting cash in each envelope—according to priority and what you most immediately need to
fund—until you run out of money.

You farm out every dollar to some purpose including necessary
expenses, living and fun expenses, savings, etc.—until every dollar is in a cubby. The thought here is that you leave no dollar
aimless. No dollar left behind, friends! If you had instead run
out of money and still had expenses to fund before you get
more money, you'd need to pull money out of an already-funded
"envelope" or figure out how else to cover it before you get more
money.

When you spend, you essentially take money out of the appro-
priate envelope. Each envelope is the equivalent of a category

in your budget. If you never spend any money in that category, that envelope will have exactly the same amount of money next month and next month, all the way into the sunset.

You don't keep a tally of the amounts in all the envelopes and let *that* number inform your spending; you rather look in the envelope for that category to tell you what you have available to spend. If something unexpected comes up, or you want to overspend on a category, you simply need to pull money from another envelope to cover it.

I affectionately refer to this shift as "breaking up with your checking account balance" and it's a game-changer for those who, like I used to, think that plenty of money in Checking means you have plenty to spend.

Now feels like a great time to check in with you, and see how you're feeling. If you're feeling anxious or stressed, that is not your cue to close the book and return to business-as-usual. Remember that spending-as-usual is not stress-free territory, and that there is no judgment in this book—just hope and help from someone who made a royal mess with money for a very long time.

BENEFITS OF ZERO-BASED BUDGETING

Zero-based budgeting, or what I will simply refer to as "budgeting" in this book, has the following benefits:

- It gives guardrails for spending decisions.

- It keeps your money clearly organized from week to week and month to month.

- Account balances no longer inaccurately inform spending decisions.

- It gives you the chance to clean up moments of over-spending as they happen.

Can you see how these would be helpful? And why what you've been doing has maybe not worked, or worked very well? If I've done my job, you're still with me and catching a glimpse of how money can be different for you. You've seen yourself in some of the anecdotes and mindsets that I've shared and can see how maybe you are not fatally flawed when it comes to money!

> NOTE: I've created a checklist you can use whenever you're ready to create and use this kind of budget. We don't dive into the *doing* until Part 3, but you may want to access it now to have it handy. Visit emilyburnett.me /spender to get this checklist and other related resources.

Throughout Part 1, I've shared my story to encourage readers that if I—a lover of nice things, and a non-frugalista—could fall in love with proactive money management as an oasis of control and the means by which I could afford a beautiful life, anyone can. Feelings of shame, stress, embarrassment, and being behind in life can be behind you.

But there's even more! I'd be no kind of money BFF if I left you here. Now that the pump has been primed, it's time to dive further into seven specific benefits of positive budgeting you can look forward to.

PART 2: THE BENEFITS

With the stage for budgeting now set, there are seven specific benefits I am excited to delve into. You are hopefully feeling at least a little jazzed about what you've read so far, and these next chapters are meant to be a major shot of adrenaline in the managing-money-in-this-way direction.

And that way, when you get to Part 3 (the actual doing), you'll be beyond ready to jump in and *do*. Let's just get the rest of your motivation on board before jumping into that, since with your motivation fully on board, you'll be able to embrace intentional money for keeps, and not as a passing fancy.

Chapter 5

MORE GOOD THINGS

A favorite fridge magnet reads, "I just cleaned under the couch cushions, and it turns out I'm queen of quite a lot." This magnet maker totally understands my childhood experiences.

My grandparents bequeathed my parents a matching brown tweed furniture set at some point during my childhood. I remember spending hours reading in the comfort of the—by that point—threadbare brown tweed couch and rocker. It was on the brown tweed couch that I completed hours of high school homework while my younger brother lolled about on the floor near it, stirring only and with stunning speed to trap my legs when I left the couch.

When things in my adolescent financial picture become really dire, I remember searching underneath these couch cushions.

Inevitably, I'd find pens—we were a big writing household—and at least some coins. Nickels, dimes, and, if I was really lucky, quarters. Keep in mind that a quarter was enough to buy a candy bar, so it was not an insignificant finding. Buying treats was a big priority in my childhood, and motivation enough to risk a look under sofa cushions never knowing what else I might find.

When I began budgeting in earnest, it was the 2015 version of finding money under the sofa cushions. Times 100. I start with this benefit because everyone can get excited about it.

> It is not much of a stretch to claim that once you get on-purpose with your money, you feel like you have—and you *actually* have—more money.

It's like most good things in life, though: There is a price to be paid to reap the rewards. You have to get fully on the ride in order to experience the thrill. I'm looking at you, (formerly) Space Mountain.

If you never get on the ride, you will never know the absolute glee induced by it. There's a threshold to cross before you bask in the warmth of the fire. There's an admission price to be paid to access the Wynn buffet. There's a flight to be taken before you get to European castles.

I could go on with analogies, but I believe you now understand some of my favorite things. The point is that certain benefits cannot be reaped without planting and sowing the seed that yields that particular fruit. It's as if the rewards of the thing are almost protected *from* those who never take the wholehearted action.

Paradox can be defined as "a situation or statement that seems impossible or is difficult to understand because it contains two opposite facts or characteristics."[8] And holy smokes, did I experience happy, paradoxical results when I got serious about managing my money.

It felt paradoxical that when I got serious about budgeting (the thing people avoid because of its connotations of deprivation) and paying off debt, my life got richer. And I'm not talking about just figuratively. In even the first month or two, I discovered that I very literally had more dollars in my budget and my life and was able to save more (for debt payoff) and spend more while spending much the same as before. Essentially, I didn't suddenly begin to live on the cheap to free up money. So the circumstance of saving more and spending more should not have been simultaneously true, and had not been in the past.

WHAT'S POSSIBLE FOR WELL-MANAGED MONEY

Where had all this extra money been going before? It was as if dollars were literally wandering away, since I wasn't doing a great job of planning them.

Says Stephen Hawking in *A Brief History of Time*, "It is a matter of common experience that disorder will tend to increase if things are left to themselves."[9] Nowhere is this more true than with money.

My financial priorities were now the following, in this order:

1. Save $1,000, and only $1,000.

2. Pay down my smallest debt ASAP, then the second, etc.

Armed with a happy dose of reality, a plan, and a real, living budget, I was shocked by how quickly I was able to hit the first goal and move into the second, while setting aside modest amounts of money in budget categories such as "Clothing & Luxuries" and "Entertainment." I was proactively planning for things I had not factored into my equation before, preferring instead to think unhelpful things like, "I actually don't buy clothes" or, "I don't really take vacations." These were big fat lies:-) And I was done telling them to myself.

So here I was, making more tangible and rapid progress than literally ever before on my goals toward financial freedom. *And* I felt like I was spending more on some of the cushier parts of life, only now guilt-free since I had planned on it. I tried to wrap my head around the mathematical equation that seemed inexplicably true: $1+1 = 3$.

The only logical conclusion was that my half-hearted attempts to budget in the past were allowing dollars to run amuck and spend themselves. Similar to the way young kids wander after churros and souvenirs and the funnest rides at a carnival, my dollars were positively wandering away. Exactly where, I couldn't have told you. I apparently wasn't paying attention.

The victims in the above scenario were my sense of confidence and the bigger dreams I had for my life. And the same may be true for you. Our dream funds never start. Or they are depleted by a lot of who-knows-exactly-what.

You over-order at a restaurant to impress the table. You impulsively add something to your cart on Amazon based solely on reviews and a "justified" emotional need. You don't realize your internet bill was higher than usual and then don't feel like making the effort to get it straightened out. Or, maybe you don't plan out your groceries very well and end up overbuying and overspending. It's $6 here and $25 there and $13 in the middle and maybe an unexpected $50 tomorrow. These small amounts of money really, really add up, falling into the figurative sofa cushions. And at the end of six months, your dream or goal is as far away as ever. When this continues to happen, you trust and like yourself less. And you add a tally mark to your mental blackboard under the heading, "I am terrible with money and this is the way I must live forever." It's a sad heading to live under. I know.

Jill came to me wanting to get serious about budgeting. She was ah, unenthused, about my recommendation to surface her true cost of living to understand the big picture of her monthly situation. And because it is imperative that the client calls the shots in a coaching relationship, I didn't press.

Fast forward three months and she was frustrated with her lack of progress in budgeting. Without question, some progress had been made, but it was slower than she wanted. And so I asked her to humor me by doing an exercise to get an approximation of her living expenses.

We did this together, and only then compared it to her monthly income. She was shocked. Not only was she not breaking even, but she saw that she could have hundreds of dollars per month to play with, and this was even estimating her expenses—her wants and her needs—high.

Without this insight, she didn't have much motivation to plan her money well (budget). And those hundreds of dollars did a marvelous job of spending themselves. The problem in this scenario is that she wasn't even able to enjoy that spending—it was stress shopping, and the kind that reinforced her belief that she was "bad with money." Getting honest about your spending, then creating a proactive budget provides a tangible and practical approach to planning and organizing your money. This ultimately helps you get organized with the fundamentals of your money. And everyone knows that it's harder to lose stuff in an organized system.

It's the equivalent of getting everything out of the corners, out from under the rug, and sweeping so you can put everything back in a nice, neat place with no question marks about what's hiding underneath. When you do this, you don't lose your favorite shirt or watch (i.e. monies) in the mess! I swear, money has a way of walking away when you don't watch it, and when you do organize and observe it, it behaves.

MONEY JUST MIGHT BE WAITING TO COME YOUR WAY

Not only will you *feel* like you have more money; you will almost certainly start *getting* more money. It's as if money waits to come to a home where it knows it will not get lost. Surprise bonuses at work, raises, surprise refunds for overpayment, a larger than projected tax refund, unexpected generosity from others.

These were all things I experienced after I began budgeting in earnest. The check I received from my insurance company for a premium refund? I almost ripped it up thinking it was just a boring Privacy Statement I most certainly didn't need to keep. I had begun tearing the envelope—my homemade form of shredding—when I decided to look at it first. Dear State Farm sent me a premium overpayment refund of $100+ for some reason I couldn't quite understand but wasn't going to argue too hard with.

It's one of the most rewarding things a client can share with me, that something financially sweet has randomly "come her way." One client, Ann, felt like she was able to spend the same amount of money and finally pay off debts one by one which brought more money into her life. She also returned to school for a master's degree, and had a realistic and awesome plan to cash-flow it. Wahoo! You can imagine her delight when she then unexpectedly received a scholarship covering half her education.

This is just one example of the wonderful things that start inexplicably coming your way as you get on-purpose with your spending. And I start this section of the book with this very practical benefit of getting intentional with money since it may be the most compelling.

Especially if things have been feeling so tight for so long, and more money feels like the answer, this is the way to 1) make more out of your current money so it feels like you are "spending more *and* saving more" and 2) set yourself up to receive more money.

When there are fewer cracks for your present money to fall through, future money also knows it will be appreciated and put to worthwhile use in your life.

Chapter 6

FINANCIAL CLARITY

Whether you wear prescription glasses or even occasional sunglasses, we've all had the experience of a smudged view. You may have gotten used to the grime on your house's windows or your car windshield. Often, we are unaware of just how dirty it is, until it's clean.

For weeks, I looked at my balcony door window and thought, "I should clean that." And also for weeks, my next thought was, "maybe it's not actually dirty and that's just the way the glass looks." I know, I know. Totally illogical, or just lazy.

One night I finally pulled out the Windex and spent all of *two minutes* cleaning it. And what do you know? It was definitely dirty. And looked infinitely better for the few minutes of effort. Newly added to my list of favorite hobbies was keeping that window clean so I could enjoy a clear view.

GETTING IT CLEAR AND KEEPING IT CLEAR

You're probably seeing where I'm going with this. When I started proactively managing my money, for genuinely the first time in my life, I could see my money situation clearly. I had all my debts in the glorious wide open and was completely honest with myself about how much I was currently spending. No more hiding behind vague categories and lumped-together, underestimated, and approximated amounts. And no more pretending I didn't spend in the categories I didn't want to admit even to myself.

Additionally, I had a system for keeping it all crystal clear. This new system replaced my system of mental juggling and good intentions I'd operated on before. It put me—the version of me with big goals and plans for life—in charge, and equipped me with real-time information with which to make decisions. If I overspent, I could see that—and fix it—immediately, instead of having it derail all my other plans for the month.

Picture a person trying to walk in a straight line from Point A to a distant Point B. If that person deviates by just 1 degree, they don't appear to be very far off course at first. But if that course is not corrected over some distance, they will end up miles away from their destination.

Similarly, many people set financial goals for the month and resolve to not overspend. They set their direction for the month.

But, largely because they do not have a system that facilitates it, they don't see clearly when they overspend.

Without noticing these mistakes, they do not have the crystal clear opportunity to fix the overspending and get back on track. In this way, they end the month overspent, stressed, and needing to pull out money that was only recently put into savings to cover the accumulated overspending of the month.

The clarity of a proactive budget empowers you to make small course corrections throughout the month. You can see very accurately what money is allocated to what purposes, and thus your spending and adjustment decisions are much clearer. You also gain clarity and visibility for your big picture— your financial goals. For the first time, you can allocate money to your goals in order of priority and watch it stay there.

When I got on purpose with my monthly money, you'll remember from the previous chapter that I:

1. Saved a modest amount that could serve as my new buffer between emergencies and my money.

2. Mapped out my debts smallest to largest and paid off the first, then second, etc. The approach of adding the payment of the first debt to the second, and so on, is often called a "debt snowball."

Before this, I practiced a very sophisticated strategy of progress called: "Do All the Good Things."

- I paid extra on some of my debts as allowed by my spending.

- I invested a modest percentage in retirement.

- I put whatever money I thought was extra in "savings."

- I was careful with my spending. Or so I thought.

However, since my spending wasn't planned or managed, the extra debt payments were sometimes the equivalent of robbing Peter to pay Paul. And what I thought was extra had actually gone to pay Mary earlier in the month.

I couldn't technically afford even the small contributions I was making to retirement. "Savings" was more a figment of my imagination because it was really just an oft-accessed, back-up checking account that covered my poor planning.

And I only *thought* I was careful with my spending. It turns out this was in theory only and occurred in fits and starts. You know that adage: "Two steps forward, one step back"? Well, I lived something like "Two steps forward, eight steps back, then one step forward, and three steps back."

I did not feel like I could impact my future, and subconsciously believed that the only solution was an unexpected and really large infusion of cash into my life. Talk about feeling the opposite of empowered! I had disempowered myself from doing anything different, and put the answer outside of my control.

A PURPOSE AND A SYSTEM

By approaching my money in this new way, for the first time I was empowered with a purpose for my money and a system to make it happen. And, critically, I knew my honest-to-goodness numbers, and had a proactive budget that would keep my plans and money organized. It all became so simple, so clear. And the feeling was a confident one of, "Oh! I can totally do *this next thing*." It didn't matter anymore what others were doing or how they were going about their financial lives.

I no longer noticed or really cared that I was years behind peers with enormous retirement and investment accounts, lovely homes, and exotic travels abroad every year under their belts. After years of comparison and coming up short, I felt liberated and in charge of my life. I was marching confidently toward *my* purpose without the confusion and overwhelm of the past.

If you've never (or never consistently) approached money like I'm describing in this book, this is the exact opposite feeling you would've expected me to have. One reason so many avoid written budgeting is that they feel like it would prevent them from buying or doing or having fun things. You might even feel like "getting on a budget" is the equivalent of admitting defeat, and that empowerment is only available when you get more money.

You may be as well-acquainted as I was with the emotions that follow a disorganized approach to money: guilt, shame, feeling out-of-control financially. In a burst of proclaimed self-care, you might do a wee bit of "retail therapy" and get an initial hit of faux-empowerment, followed hours or days later by feelings of guilt and then stress.

Note: Credit cards do a lovely job of facilitating this cycle, because you can always put your reckoning with yourself and your debt off into the future. And in that future you like to picture yourself with more money that will have fixed the problems.

I've seen clients experience wonderful benefits when they get really clear about their money:

- Cash-flowing grad school

- Seeing that they actually could leave their job and switch to freelancing

- Having a clear path to debt-freedom

- Having a path to minimize school debt and live on current income

- Realizing an emergency fund is their main goal, then having it available to cover an emergency car repair

- Budgeting for their side business

- Knowing that they can live on less if they have to

- Having more constructive conversations with their spouse about money

For many clients, they're still getting clear on their financial and life goals, and simply creating an approach to managing their finances is the biggest win.

Once I got crystal clear on the realities of my financial life, stressful thoughts like, "Dang...probably shouldn't have bought that," were immediately replaced with feelings like, "Oh yeah, baby. I just bought that [insert the fun or necessary thing you just bought] *and* everything else in my financial life is unaffected by this purchase because I planned for it."

I felt powerful with my money and choices for the first time, and oddly excited about the challenge to pay off the dang debt I'd acquired. A large part of that excitement was probably fueled by the feeling of gratitude to finally be in control of my money. And even as the novelty of these feelings wore off, the sense of empowerment never did.

The definition of empowerment I like best comes from the Cambridge dictionary: "The process of gaining freedom and power to do what you want or to control what happens to you ."[10] Is that not amazing?!

Controlling the currency of life (money) is one major way you gain that power. No more trampling on your own freedom by ignoring what you do with money! You now have a say in that currency system for which we trade our time and energy.

This is a bold assertion, but I am going to make it nonetheless: If you have been a financial mess your whole life, getting in the figurative driver's seat and buckling in by budgeting in earnest will give you more purpose and power in life than you could ever get by reading every self-help book on the market.

> Budgeting and planning your money is one of the quickest and most tangible ways to infuse your life with power.

You may not have unlimited money at your disposal, but you can control what you do with it. You can control how you manage it. You can choose to do something to increase your income. You can choose to spend differently. But only when you have a system that keeps your money organized and all your spending decisions out in the open. The clarity that follows keeps you empowered to make decisions for your life.

I started this chapter talking about a clean balcony window, and it feels only right to wrap up with talking about another window. The window we all stare out of most often is the windshield of a car, and we can all appreciate how dirty those get, inside and out. The difference between my balcony window and the windshield of a car is that the latter is what we look out of en route to our destinations.

Considering a new approach to money—and finally budgeting in a way that works—can give you immense clarity en route to your bigger life goals. The cleaner that windshield, the more actual and figurative clarity you'll enjoy.

Chapter 7

FREEDOM

I n *The Power of Habit*, author Charles Duhigg relates the story of a woman who underwent a radical change over the course of just months. At the start of the year, she is a mess—a chain smoker, coming out of a messy divorce, financially broke, nonskilled, overweight, and out of shape. Just two years later, she quit smoking, started running marathons, retooled her career, and drastically increased her income.[11] There were no bars surrounding this woman, imprisoning her where she unhappily began the story. And yet, she had been living as a captive for years. Captive to her addiction of smoking, captive to the effects of low self-worth, captive to her financial situation of low income and poor spending.

FREEDOM OF CHOICE

Most humans technically have the power of choice. But we do a marvelous job of limiting our personal freedom of choice. It's not all our own doing, however. Statista.org estimates that, by

2024, media advertising spending in the U.S. will reach $322 billion.[12] That's a lot of dollars behind companies and products telling you that you need to buy X and do Y in order to be happier!

Stoicism is a Greek school of philosophy known for its focus on the pursuit of key virtues such as courage, temperance, justice and wisdom. To some, this philosophy can appear unfeeling or cold in its detachment from possessions and even relationships. That aside, if we were all Stoics, we would be immune from the efforts of marketers. But we're not, and human desire, combined with the inclination to compare ourselves and circumstances to whatever those dang Joneses are doing certainly does not set us up for a life of reason and responsibility.

And we can find ourselves driven about, as it were, in a monetary game of getting and having. Not exactly wanting the result of being trapped in careers we don't like, homes and cars and degrees we can't afford, and living a life below our potential, but finding ourselves there nonetheless.

How to counter this enslavement? Become the boss of your money and what you do with it. Do you have plans for your life? I sure do. Land in Montana, annual writing trips to Ireland, charitable causes to support, additional degrees I want to earn, etc. What are some of yours?

Do you sincerely want your current circumstances to stretch into perpetuity unchanged? I doubt that. And if you do, congratulations on either being really content or having gotten it all figured out early. If you're reading this book, however, I suspect you feel stuck. Trapped. Limited in your options.

What does every single one of our plans require? You got it. Money. Money and character and perseverance and discipline and good habits and intentional living. But since this is a book about budgeting, we'll focus on the money required for every life goal.

Even if one of your goals is to volunteer at a vegan, organic farm on the Oregon Coast for a year, you need to have your money in order. Unless you are independently wealthy, at least a few bills will need to be paid during this meatless, cheese-less year. You'll probably still have some gifts you'd like to give, and social activities requiring money. And, when the dairy-free year is over, you'll need to have money to return to normal life.

Freedom in the financial sense means you have options. Only by getting your money organized can you do things like eliminate debt, spend in a way that doesn't jeopardize all of your future plans, and stay free.

Free to do what? Pursue new career and hobby opportunities, move to new places, and try new things. Quit the job you loathe and volunteer in refugee camps for a year. Financially support causes you care about. Be generous to friends and family in hard times. Buy land. Take classes. Yes, people have done all these things with and while in debt. But significantly more have felt as stuck as I did, limited from opportunities by the circumstances I'd put myself in.

Without the load of debt or poor spending and the accompanying feeling of guilt, shame, and complacency, you are for the first time free to explore and choose your path.

When I graduated college, I should have launched into a wonderful, empowered, choose-my-own-adventure chapter. But I didn't. I had two credit cards with balances in the thousands of dollars. I had student loans that would soon enter repayment. I had a car payment for my new-to-me 1998 Toyota Corolla—white, for your information, and despite what the used car salesman said, I am nearly positive it had been smoked in. I blame no one but myself and poor decision-making and planning for the debt I carried.

I had earned a college degree that had taught me a lot and which has proved to be a great foundation for life. But it didn't exactly set me apart in my job search. Let's just say decent-paying jobs were not knocking down my door upon college graduation. I moved home—thanks for the free rent, Mom and Dad!—while I waited to hear back on my PA school applications. After a month-long job search, I found a fun hourly job and made enough to scrape by. I certainly was not making enough to set sail anywhere fast except across the pond in my parent's neighborhood.

This trend of scraping-by continued even after I didn't get into PA school. In hindsight, I wonder what my debt load would have been like had I gotten in since I had no money saved up for it. I had big dreams but only chased them with debt because I wasn't able to chase them any other way. Or so I thought.

My choices had led to being buried in debt. When I finally chose to get out of debt, learning how to plan and budget my money, I found myself luxuriating in choices, in options. I now had the opportunity to think through existential big-picture questions. I didn't really need my current salary and could live my existing life on less than half of it. If I had wanted to do something really crazy like quit my job and join the Peace Corp, I could've afforded to for as long as my savings would last.

I could mow lawns 20 hours a week. I could work at Costco. I could paint houses. I could move across the country. I could live in a tent in Colorado, work 10 hours a week at a bakery and spend the rest of my time reading, volunteering, etc. I didn't do any of those things, but the point is that unique situations like these were options I could viably consider for the first time in my life. My expenses were low, I had no debt, and I had a money system that would help me manage any amount of money, large or small.

FREEDOM FROM DEBT

The opposite of freedom is bondage or restriction. When you are in debt or when your money is spending you instead of the other way around, you are restricted. The incredibly accessible credit system gives you a false or temporary sense of freedom to take that trip of a lifetime, buy the boat, live more expensively than your income allows.

But most people's relationship using debt is a bit like a game of Monopoly. It includes a Get Out of Jail card, but this card functions a bit differently than you're used to.

In this Monopoly life, imagine you have a prison sentence of five years, but you can take leave any time you want. The caveat? Your sentence is extended by 2.5x the amount of leave you take. So you take a month off. It feels awesome. But by doing so, you added two and a half months to the end of your sentence.

You return to prison and tell yourself that you're not going to do that ever again; nope, never! You're going to hunker down and plow through your sentence. But something comes up and you take a week away. That week away tacks an additional two and half weeks on to your already extended sentence. Two months away for a family thing adds five months to your sentence. And so on.

A five-year sentence becomes a six-year sentence, and that extends to eight years. But nearly everyone you know is doing it, so it really doesn't seem like *that* big of a deal. Sure, it'd be nice to not return there, but you've gotten kind of used to it, it's not that bad, and is there really much you can do about it?

And then one day, you realize something. You don't have to spend a day longer than your sentence, and in fact, you can shorten your sentence. The fine print of this hypothetical prison sentence says something about earning time off for good be-havior. You can deduct time for doing certain things, which are—coincidentally—intrinsically satisfying.

And so you start. Your now eight-year sentence drops quickly to seven years, then five, then four, then three, and you walk out the doors in two, resolved never to return. Your temporary furloughs of fake freedom never felt this good, this lasting. And because you have developed the solid habits that have led to your early release, you know it is within your control never to return.

Breaking up with debt is similar. If you've been in debt, you realize how it actually did not serve you. The debt I'm speaking of is the kind that allows you to delay consequences or avoid facing reality, not the reasonable debt used to do reasonable things like purchase a home within your means or fund reasonable and known education costs.

Some people are able to use debt responsibly, and if used in con-junction with a living, breathing budget system, you can come pretty close to a "plan now, buy now" life. Where you plan your spending using real money, spend according to that plan, and move the money to a category to pay off the spending at the end of the month. Notice that the credit cards don't float you in the same way that most people use them. The way most people use them, and certainly the way I used them, reminds me of a monkey trap.

In case you're unfamiliar with a monkey trap, picture this: Some-thing a monkey wants, like a nut, is placed inside a container or gourd with a hole just small enough for their hand to pass through unclenched. When their fist is clenched and full of the thing they want, they are unable to withdraw their hand. And it's called a trap because they often opt to be captured or killed instead of letting go of the nut.

I suppose it's possible a few animals are lucky enough to get the reward in the trap without getting caught. Some are disciplined enough to give up the nut in order to withdraw their hand, but these would be the exception. Credit cards can be like the monkey trap. Some people are able to use them without getting trapped into overspending and carrying balances, but these people are the exception.

I was not the exception. I wanted the nut (immediate purchasing power, delayed spending consequences) and my freedom too. But I only got one of the two. So even though my jail-sentence analogy above is totally fictitious, I can relate in a small way to the restriction on freedom.

Bondage looks like not being able to speak for all of your money because various creditors and past decisions have their fingers in your pie. Or, if you have miraculously avoided debt despite your financial management habits, bondage is a feeling of being stuck. A feeling that nothing you do will yield a brighter future. It's making ends meet just enough that you don't feel you can choose which jobs you take, where you live, what hobbies you can pursue, how you can help others, what emergencies you can deal with.

If you are mired in debt, yo-yoing between binge cycles of credit card debt, or find yourself perpetually stressed and stretched by just how many financial emergencies happen— Christmas, car repairs, taxes, car insurance premiums every 6 months, Amazon Prime membership, braces for kids—you may feel like you're successfully walking a 2x4 balance beam until one of these emergencies comes and gives you a shove. But are any of these actually "emergencies"?

There may be a few car repairs that are actually emergencies. An engine going out or hitting debris on the freeway which hurts the car's underside (can you tell I'm not a car expert?) or sliding on icy roads can incur thousands of dollars of body damage rendering your non-comprehensively insured car inoperable until fixed.

There are things that break in homes that you really couldn't plan for and have to be fixed.

You could face medical costs that either aren't covered by insurance or that incur a large out-of-pocket expense. Emergencies do happen. However, Christmas is on the calendar every single year.

You know that, even if you pay your car insurance premium every 6 months, it does have a monthly cost breakdown and you could treat it like a monthly bill to be "paid." Similarly, Amazon Prime has a monthly cost even if you pay annually.

You can estimate your taxes and do some educated guessing about your exemptions.

You may not know which car repairs are coming, or which things in the house will need attention, or anticipate specific sicknesses or injuries, but you can know that some of them are coming.

Once you get out of debt, the figurative balance beam gets a lot wider. For one, you don't have the same monthly payments that kept you living on the edge financially. Second, as you budget and spend within your income, you can see much more clearly the edges of your balance beam and how you can make it wider.

At my second peak of debt I had a portfolio of credit card, student loan, and auto loan debt of $48,000. This meant I had to pay $1,050 minimum every single month for things in my past. The enjoyment of most of the purchases was in my past and I truly was paying for it (plus interest) now.

Let's break that down a little bit more. Let's estimate an hourly equivalent wage of $40. This becomes $30 after taxes.

$1,050 divided by $30 is 35 hours every single month being required to pay for past decisions. That's nearly a week of full time work just to pay off my past. The other three weeks' wages were available to pay for my current and future life. By paying off all my debt, I freed up the $1,050 to be available for my future life, my dreams and hopes and plans. Talk about freedom, baby! Sure, my plans were still limited by reality and what I was willing to spend my money on, but to not have to pay so much to my past gave my dreams and plans wings.

I think about a favorite game growing up, "Capture the Flag." In this game, you have two goals: First, find your flag hidden on the other team's side, and second, get your team members out of jail so they can help find the flag.

Getting a handle on your finances is a bit like getting *yourself* out of jail to be free to pursue your potential. You are the one trusted with your life—no one else. You might get rescued by some sweet payout, but that won't change you in the way that you most need changing. Start acting like your life is worth improving—it is—and that you are worth it—you are!

You can't help the world when you're stuck and not free. Reading about Operation Underground Railroad—a nonprofit dedicated to rescuing children from sex trafficking—for the first time, I could actually respond. I could make regular donations from real money, not debt. I could quit my job and work for them for a modest hourly rate. I didn't quit my job, but the point is that you can respond to causes and opportunities readily when you're not trapped under a pile of dumb rocks that you piled on top of yourself.

FREEDOM FROM SHAME

In addition to the practical benefits of being free (freed up money, more options in life), you also get a powerful feeling of freedom when all money things are out in the open. No more hiding in shame. No more hiding receipts, transactions, and debt balances from your significant other or dating prospects. No more buying shiny stuff to impress people who will not even notice or be impressed.

Freedom in this sense refers to the freedom from oppressive things you've gotten used to living with: guilt, shame, and hiding.

You also will experience more freedom from the pressuring and incessant ploys of marketers. I worked in marketing for a decade. In one of my roles, I managed the team sending batches of millions of marketing emails telling our customers and prospective customers what they should buy from us BECAUSE IT'S ON SALE and BECAUSE YOUR LIFE IS DRAB WITHOUT IT and BECAUSE EVERYONE ELSE HAS IT. Okay, okay. We never sent emails with such blatant messages, but this is the tone of most marketing messages. Am I right?

We sent millions of emails and an average consumer was emailed dozens of times a year by just our company. Internet ads, Pandora and Spotify ads, ads on podcasts, car wraps, billboards, branding on cycling jerseys; marketing is everywhere. Speaking of cycling jerseys, can you please explain to me how literally every cyclist seems to be affiliated with a sponsoring company? Is it a universal law that no jersey can be sponsor-free or do cyclists just not wear them?

There is no definitive average number of advertising messages we are exposed to each day, but a quick Google search suggests it's in the thousands. All the way back in 2007, one New York Times article estimated the number of ad messages seen per *day* by a person living in a city to be 5,000.[13] Whatever the actual number, there's no question we all have a lot of inputs. Your exposure to marketing messages, of course, correlates to your habits and routines. But it's impossible to be a functioning member of society and not see at least dozens every day.

As a baked goods fan, I think the marketing ploy behind this anecdote is genius and hilarious: "Last month, after some "Got Milk?" billboards started emitting the odor of chocolate chip cookies at San Francisco bus stops, many people complained, and the city told the California Milk Processing Board to turn off the smell."[14] And even though I'm only reading and writing about this happening, I—miles and years away from the incident—suddenly have the urge to eat chocolate chip cookies and milk. You, too?

I have a favorite *I Love Lucy* episode called "Sales Resistance." If you know Lucy, you know that she perpetually overspends and her household accounts are frequently overdrawn. In this particular episode, Lucy tries unsuccessfully to not be persuaded by the salesman's pitch for the Handy-Dandy Vacuum Cleaner.

But said salesman appeals to her vanity, convinces her that her life will be vastly improved by this vacuum, and generally encourages her to buy the vacuum she really doesn't need and certainly can't afford. (It ends up being a dud, and she tries so hard to return it to the aggressive salesman. Fails. Then, after Ricky gives her a hard time for being unable to resist or return the appliance, he also proves unable. It's awesome.)

Even if you do not live in the city or do not consume as many advertising opportunities as others, we can all agree that there are a lot of invitations to buy, do, consume, and want "stuff " that companies or neighbors or family members want us to. Companies talk about being "customer obsessed" which usually means they want to profile customers so that they know how to sell more stuff to them.

Anyway, when you take control of your money, you will be more aware of what money you spend and where. And it will make you more "sales resistant." Just because something is on sale does not mean it fits into your budget or your plan for your money or life. Thirty percent off a $200 pair of jeans when you have $30 in your clothing budget and no other categories you want to deplete is still $110 out of your budget. And that's okay! Remember, you created this plan for yourself, and you had good reasons for it.

For further assistance in saying no to things that formerly derailed your finances, try on this thought: You were okay with yourself and your life before you saw the advertisement or the sale, weren't you?

Knowing exactly how much money you have and spending within it is freedom from the subtle or direct messages of companies or others in your life who want you to keep affording what you are affording, or spend more, or spend more like them. None of these companies or friends with plans for your money are magically depositing money into your checking account to cover payment for any of the things they pressure you to buy. And if they are, please tell me how you worked that out.

By the end of this chapter, I hope you are as excited as I am about what you might do with more freedom. You may not immediately be completely financially free to pursue your exciting goals, but can see that more freedom is totally possible for you. Your previously impossible goal of debt-freedom becomes wonderfully possible, and you are incredibly motivated by the "raise" you'll give yourself when you're out from under it. And those yucky feelings of shame and pressure? A freer you is in charge and calling the shots now. All these types of freedom and more are possible as you get—and stay—in charge of your money.

Chapter 8

PROGRESS

I love business. From my childhood, I have loved the concept that you can make something or offer a service, and people will pay you for it. And if you make or offer something people really want, lots of them will pay you lots of money for it. This has led me to create or participate in multiple side businesses. If you include all my childhood business, we're probably looking at a baker's dozen (13). That does include promising ventures like "Cozy Corner," a cafe my siblings and I managed in our childhood home. Mom and Dad ate a lot of cinnamon toast, our specialty.

My dad ran his own successful company until he retired in his early fifties. My grandfather was a beloved 5th-grade math teacher and endless dabbler in businesses, some with my grandmother—who was a side hustler in her own right.

Some of their business ventures include collecting insects for biological weed control—a lucrative, seasonal, and very unglamorous business that blessed my high school life—a downtown bakery in Bozeman, Montana, and a sawmill that probably never made them money but gave Grandpa endless pleasure preparing his own lumber. And gave us grandkids endless pleasure by clamoring all over the machine. Safe? Doubtful. Memorable? Definitely.

What on earth do any of these stories have to do with money and why are they in a book about budgeting? Well, in every instance, these business ventures were an attempt to build something, to make progress and maximize independence, and enjoying the process of doing so. The process of building something and working toward something was an immense source of satisfaction to my grandpa, even before the aim was achieved. And approaching your money situation with proactive and happy budgeting can do the same thing for you.

> "When you fall in love with the process rather than the product, you don't have to wait to give yourself permission to be happy. You can be satisfied anytime your system is running."[15]
>
> James Clear

I've shared earlier in the book that, when I finally and firmly embarked on a new chapter of budgeting and planning my money, all my feelings about money did an about-face. I still had months and years to go to have my debt paid off. So why did I suddenly feel so dang good about myself and my money?

It's because, as much as I wanted the product of becoming debt-free, I had fallen in love with having a *system* that was working. I loved the direction I was heading, and had "fallen in love with the process." Without question, I knew that the process would be the vehicle of progress.

The word "validate" often applies to someone other than ourselves showing approval for something we're doing. A boss validates an idea at work. A parent validates a child's choice. A friend validates a decision as "a good idea." Some external validation is unsolicited, but you may also be in a habit of asking others if your decisions are acceptable. You may never have turned inward and validated your own decisions.

Getting on purpose with my money was followed immediately by a feeling of "rightness," that I liked the decisions I was making and, while most responsible people would too, I didn't need their approval like I had before. Since I felt deep into my gut that my decisions were taking me places I wanted to go, I needed validation from others much less. And keeping up with the elusive Joneses? That mattered so much less.

INEVITABLE PROGRESS

You'll love this feeling of knowing that you are *finally* and *actually* making progress. Even before you get to the destination. For someone honestly budgeting, progress, even if small at first, is inevitable. Especially if you've been a yo-yoer in finances, lifestyle habits, career exploration, you will revel in the feeling of tangible progression. You can see the ball moving forward toward the goal line.

This feeling is super sustaining when the inevitable, temporary setbacks occur. Car repairs, fixing home appliances, medical happenings. Knowing you have a system that supports you in this Adventure of Progress, and that you can get back on the horse anytime you fall off, means you can be content and have that feeling of rightness, simply because your system is running.

There is so much in life that is outside our control: dating relationships, natural disasters, friendships, family situations, the stock market, decisions made by executives at your company, health, etc. And it can sometimes be really hard to feel like you are making progress or that your actions matter.

Take a career for example: You might have a job you like fine but are not sure what you want to do with it. You may not be all that jazzed about any of the options you see for promotion but don't know what else you'd pursue. You feel stagnant, like you're missing a sense of forward motion in your life but aren't sure which direction to head.

I was here several years ago. I'd been with my job for three years, the first two of which were filled with learning and growth. However, that third year I felt utterly stuck. Barring any changes above me, there wasn't a logical promotion. Raises were limited to "cost of living" salary nudges. All the learning of the first couple years resulted in me knowing my job well but not having the same opportunities for learning and growth.

This particular job was pretty black-and-white, with not a lot of room in the industry or this particular work environment for creativity or innovation. I was fresh out of a rollercoaster romantic relationship; this break-up on top of my job situation had me feeling like I was not headed anywhere. I made decent money, but it was barely enough to pay my bills, afford some fun, and make my debt payments to the tune of several hundred dollars. I had amazing friends and adventure buddies; my family has always been awesome, and that chapter for us was no different; and I was happily involved in my church community.

However, I didn't have a direction and it affected me more than I knew at the time. I only realized it once I was solidly striving toward something tangible and measurable and within my control—getting out of debt and taking the reins of my money. For you, it might be saving up for IVF, buying a house, cash-flowing grad school, etc.

YOU CAN LOVE THE DESTINATION AND THE JOURNEY

The instant you get serious about a spending plan that supports a life direction, not only do your big dreams start to feel possible, but your immediate finances also improve. You feel the marvelous feeling of progress toward both of those because, obvious alert, you are *actually making progress* toward your why's: Early retirement? Month-long scuba trip? Pay off all consumer debt? Pay off even the house early? Or, if you need to get the house first, saving for a respectable downpayment? Quit the corporate job you've never enjoyed to run your own business?

Any of these could mark progress that you've never made before. Dreamt of, sure. But seen tangible headway toward? Nope. And the results you have now are intoxicating. That feeling that what you are doing is good. And not because others are clapping and cheering for you all along the way. Some might, of course. But those who have become accustomed to you spending in a manner similar to them will be disappointed. And that's okay, your own validation matters more than validation from anyone else.

Doesn't it all sound incredibly obvious? Unfortunately, if it were, all of us would've started managing our money better years ago. It's a bit like being on a lake in a boat. Pick a boat, any boat. As long as it's a boat that you have to paddle. This is important for the analogy. Okay, so here we are. On the lake, in our paddle-able boat. We have oars.

You're looking at the shore and in every direction, there is something you could head toward, some more interesting or worthwhile than others. You may think "Gosh, I'd like to get off this lake" but not actually head toward any mark on the shore, distracted instead by the destinations of friends paddling around you.

You take a couple strokes toward one point, and look around to ask those around you if it was a good idea. "No," they say. "You should actually head 90 degrees to your left. You'll like it better. It makes more sense."

And so you pivot and start aiming toward their recommended destination. But then someone else suggests, either verbally or by example, heading back more toward the original destination, and so you paddle that way until yet a third option arises that sounds like it will be fun or boost your social status.

Sometimes you head indecisively toward a mark on the shore that looks like where you actually want to go, but change course when someone else comes by in a shinier boat. "Oooo, where are they heading? Let's go see!" Or they tell you explicitly where to go, and you do because it seems like then you'll be valid and worthwhile. Enough of these happenings and you never actually get to anything on the shore.

Counter this with you picking a spot on the shore, knowing it's a good one, and rowing with fixed determination toward it. Yes, you might get distracted by a degree or two by the priorities of other people or unexpected life happenings, but you can easily course correct since they haven't been able to change your ultimate destination, just a few paddle strokes.

Your system helps you identify the deviation from your direction, so you just simply stroke back on course, and resume making the tangible progress you've gotten used to making.

You won't ever want to go back to aimless drifting.

It may seem wild that all of this is possible simply by managing the roots of your money. And if I hadn't experienced it for myself, I might be a tad skeptical. But it is amazing how quickly you can get on-purpose and start providing your own validation. Long before you get to your longed-for destination, you can quickly fall in love with the process of getting there. No matter what anyone thinks about your new habits or spending priorities, you have your own respect in new and motivating ways.

Chapter 9

CONFIDENCE

C onfidence. We all know it when we feel it, am I right?

And how about the unpleasant opposites of feeling confident? Some of these feelings include being uncertain, doubtful, hesitant, tentative, unconvinced, indecisive, unsure, speculative, unsettled, wavering, changeable.

Any of those sound familiar?

For those of you mired in debt payments, anxiously waiting for each payday, feeling like life is just one big financial emergency after another and like you simply can't get ahead, your sense of confidence has been beaten down. It may be limited to just your personal finance, but it may extend to other areas, and you may be accepting less than you're worth, figuratively and literally.

What if the secret to gaining or regaining confidence with money has little to do with the amount of money you have, and much to do with the management of that money? Well, that is how this works.

Financial confidence flourishes when you take the reins of your money life instead of letting life happen to your money.

This is especially pertinent if you have made a mess of your money and acquired large quantities of debt. But I have also seen a lack of money organization cause enormous doubt in people making hundreds of thousands of dollars. The client making nearly $1 million made more money than any of my other clients, but his spending and behavior with money in general caused him similar, if not greater, feelings of daily stress and insecurity. When he spent, he really spent. And he really felt the stress of all the spending he and his family were doing on luxury vacations, running multiple households, and so much more.

I've deemed it a universal law that anyone spending more than they can afford is going to feel lousy about themselves. It's a subset of this law that anyone who doesn't know what they can afford is also going to feel lousy with money. Having confronted all the facts of a situation and having a written plan for spending is the key difference. The only exceptions I've seen to my expertly developed universal law are some people who are, by nature, quite frugal. That's not me, and that's probably not you either since you're reading this book.

There's a difference between those who claim they never spend money and those who really don't. A scripture in the New Testament says, "By their fruits ye shall know them."[16] Do your fruits (results) indicate you actually spend more than you say? And what are the fruits of your interactions with your money? Confident or insecure?

The good news is that feeling confident is 1000% possible even for you. Examine your habits. Unearth all your expenses. Choose what in your approach or spending patterns you want to change. Even if you feel like you only spend on what's absolutely necessary, you are short-changing yourself the feelings of confidence and assurance that come by simply adding a proactive written money plan to your life.

And then there's the category of folks who have no problem spending money, not necessarily because they have it. They spend in a big way to receive approval. Nice cars, expensive meals and vacations, big gifts, all purchased and talked about as if they're no big deal.

I know from first-hand experience what it's like to be extravagant using debt or while mired in debt. I wanted to hide my stress and less than awesome financial situation by acting like I had plenty of money and no qualms about spending it. It was easier to be a fake version of generous and confident while using fake money. It may not be as generous as it seems if it's coming from a place of seeking approval, or you genuinely shouldn't afford it.

If you think more money is the answer to your life and money problems, and that you'd surely be confident with money if you suddenly had $100,000 more in your life, think again.

In 2017 well-known actor Johnny Depp sued his managers for mismanagement of his financial affairs. They counter-sued, stating that they "did not have the power or ability to control Depp's spending or his numerous other vices, or to force Depp to make wiser financial decisions."[17]

Highlights from the list of spending decisions in the cross-complaint are remarkable to say the least. The one I have the hardest time wrapping my head around is the monthly wine bill of $30,000. I'm neither judge nor jury in this case, but I suspect I feel more empowered and confident with my money than Mr. Depp. And you can too.

CONFIDENCE IN RELATIONSHIPS

When I was nearing the climax of my debt, I dreaded conversations turning to finances—even when I had largely stopped using debt to fund vacations and business pursuits. Making no progress toward paying it off was a sore spot and a source of resistance to money talk. I was ashamed of my debt "portfolio," that I hadn't been able to buy a house yet, that my healthy income didn't quite cover my lifestyle which was, by a lot of peer standards, not extravagant at all.

Especially in dating relationships, I worried that things like debt or savings or investments would come up. To say it was a sensitive subject would be an understatement. The anxiety came from my own embarrassment about behaviors, and also because I thought

I "should" be farther along. It was a super fun game of comparison and self-shaming.

Every time someone would compliment me on my well-maintained Honda CRV (which I had bought, with a loan, brand new at a time when the cost of the car was almost equal to my salary) I'd worry about follow-up questions. Not sure why. Well, actually, I do know why. I'd had people ask about the top-of-the-line Subaru and how much I'd paid for it, followed by something additionally tactless like, "Do you have that kind of money?"

As a side-note, I probably didn't need to be as insecure as I was. According to Bankrate, in 2023 the average car payment for a new vehicle is $716. The same article highlights that in 2022, 80 .9% of new cars were purchased with financing.[18] And according to a 2022 Experian finding, 40% of used cars on the road are financed.[19] So I'm not sure why I would've felt insecure about having a financed car—the majority of cars are! Of course, just because everyone does it doesn't make it a strategy that engenders personal confidence.

Back to my dating history: I've had great boyfriends and been on terrible first dates and everything in between. I've had one-hour dates and nine-hour marathon dates—are you going to like *any* stranger when you spend so much concentrated time together so soon? I've gone out with short guys, tall guys, handsome guys, and some really nice guys that were...less my type. The one thing that was consistent throughout my dating career (pre-debt-pay-off) was my sense of shame about my financial predicament. Basically, I was insecure about my financial situation, my behaviors, and my future prospects, and didn't want guys to know about it.

Some of the guys I dated were what we might call "loaded." With them I always felt a sense of imbalance, that they'd done so well and applied themselves to saving and investing and being smart with their money. I know now that I gave some of them a little or a lot too much figurative credit. I gauged our financial differences to be wider than they actually were. Oh the assumptions you make when confidence is low!

I also knew I didn't want a guy or anyone else to rescue me from the dumb decisions and spending choices I had made. It felt too easy. Like I wouldn't have the satisfaction of cleaning up my years of poor planning. I believed deep down that the right guy would be willing to move forward in a relationship with me despite my financial mess, and I had conversations with a couple of serious boyfriends validating this belief—the right guy wouldn't walk away from the right relationship due solely to debt and poor planning. But still, I didn't want to put that burden on anyone else.

There were, however, several more guys that I never talked about money with. Or if I did, it was superficial or even evasive. Some of that is just smart; you don't want to share too much too soon with just anyone. You know? But even with those I spent more time with, I didn't want to tell them that I had debt, much less tell them I had student loan debt from my bachelor's degree a decade earlier from an inexpensive but prestigious university.

I didn't want them to know I had credit card debt or a car loan and very little savings. And so whenever money came up I would just change the subject or not engage deeper. And yet, my perceived inequality in our money situation would be a wedge between us. Again, I probably gave too many of them way too much figurative credit, and myself not enough. The statistics are on my side in this regard.

Here's where things changed in my dating life and where Confidence makes her debut: Almost the instant I got fully on board with proactive money management, including a budget, *and* had a written, specific plan for paying off my debt, the shame and guilt melted away. I'd gotten pretty comfortable having those feelings around, but this new surge of confidence was most welcome and liberating.

I didn't have anything to hide, and was happy to tell any curious party about my financial plans. Some things are always in poor taste to talk about, like salaries and how much certain things cost, but I was no longer embarrassed about the debt I'd acquired or my previous behaviors. This because I had new behaviors and systems on my side, and had the confidence that accompanies firm resolve.

You may not be single and dating, but I suspect you can relate to my dating experiences when you consider your network of friends, family members, coworkers, and neighbors. If you've formerly hid your financial woes from the world, you'll really enjoy the liberation and confidence of knowing what your plans and your priorities are, regardless of what others are doing or buying or investing in.

Your neighbor can take the fancy trips and buy the exciting things, and you can now hear about them as something awesome for her, and something you might consider doing when it works out in your financial plans. This instead of hearing about the purchases of others with jealousy and potentially making splurge decisions to try to buy confidence in relation to others.

CONFIDENCE WITH YOURSELF

But all the above deals with external facing financial confidence, how you feel with and around others. The more important side of confidence is internal facing, however. The kind of confidence that you would have even if you were the only person on the planet. It's proving to *yourself* that you can do this, that you can be different than you have been, that you can actually trust yourself.

This is the most important aspect of confidence since your relationship with yourself is the most important thing you have in your life. Without waxing too philosophical—this is a book about money management, after all—the relationship you have with yourself projects onto all other relationships and is the foundation on which you build everything else in your life. So it really matters, and taking the reins of your money is one sure way to develop it.

"Confidence is directness and courage in meeting
the facts of life."

John Dewey

I like to think of confidence as the belief that you can rely on
someone or something. When your past experience with money
proves that you haven't been able to rely on yourself, it does not
engender self-confidence. But when you embrace budgeting and
can see your actions positively impacting your financial situation,
a healthier belief in yourself is a natural result.

The downside of poor spending—such as purchasing clothes
on credit or to the detriment of your actual expenses like Utilities or Groceries—has been a constant reminder of your lack of
discipline. It's like the wrong kind of trophy wall. Purchasing
mass quantities, buying spontaneously with no idea how it will
be afforded, or justifying expenses you know definitely can't be
afforded are motivated by some emotion: boredom, low self-esteem, or craving acceptance. This kind of spending is a hobby
with a very low barrier to entry, and a very damaging effect on
your confidence.

Confidence comes from having a plan, a system, and a very honest conversation with yourself about the realities of your life. This
confidence allows you to carry your head high even when your
clothes aren't the newest, or your car is nine years old, or you opt
not to spend as much or as often on lunches out like coworkers.
Do you even remember when most people used to work in the

same *place* as their coworkers, not wear yoga pants every day, and do things like go out for lunch together?

When I hold events, and even in one-on-one conversations with clients, confidence is one of the feelings they desire most. They want to feel confident about their financial choices and how they take care of what they earn. Only after you've experienced emotional insecurity and sometimes practical insecurity around money do you fully understand this longing.

The best news is that this confidence really is available to anyone willing to do the things that engender confidence. And that it, like the other life-changing benefits of budgeting, can come sweeping in as soon as you start managing your money in proactive ways.

Chapter 10

PEACE

"Anxiety is caused by a lack of control, organization, preparation, and action."

David Kekich

I recently enjoyed some solo travels in southern Europe. This included mostly big city experiences, lots of public transportation, and seeing famous sites. The energy of big cities like Rome is hard to beat, but after weeks of crowds, busy public transportation, and noise, I so appreciated the tranquility of things like gardens and quiet, hard-to-get-to islands.

Managing money is much the same. It's stressful to keep up with the hustle and bustle of modern life, and sometimes you don't even realize the toll it's taking on you until you experience the opposite—peace. Particularly if you've been stressed about money for some time, you're going to love this benefit. Imagine that you've been treading water in a scenic lake, just trying to keep your head above the surface. And then someone puts a platform under your feet and you can finally stop kicking and finally breathe. Ah, the sweet relief!

Before working with me, one of my clients had, a decade earlier, turned finances entirely over to her husband. Things were tight, and she thought by removing herself from the picture she would feel less stress. He was willing and ended up shouldering all of the financial management. He did his best but they weren't loving their results, which certainly included stress and mounting credit card debt. By the time they hired me as their money coach, she was ready to participate again.

During our meetings, we surfaced all their spending types and amounts. It became apparent that their spending exceeded their income by a fair amount. This reality had been masked largely by credit card use combined with variable income; it was easy to extrapolate the "high water" income months and cover the deficit on credit cards with mounting balances.

For the first time in a decade, the wife had a clear view of their tenuous financial picture, yet was able to, for the first time in years, sleep through the night. Although it was sobering to see clearly that they weren't a) consistently making enough money or b) planning it well enough to pay for their lifestyle, numerous positive things followed this reality check.

It provided an explanation for *why* they were leaning on credit cards so much and carrying balances there. It also provided an explanation for why their life *felt* tight; it was! You might be surprised to know that the feeling that accompanied this realization was actually one of marked peace.

> Surfacing all parts of your money life by getting them on paper, then getting them on purpose and on a plan has this way of cleaning the messy corners of your financial life and also of your inner life.

We acquire so much emotional baggage through what we do, acquire, and pursue as we go through life. As it relates to money, we carry around heavy burdens of stress and anxiety when we ignore our financial reality. We keep up a frantic pace of life just trying to avoid having to sort through that baggage, all the while seeking a feeling of peace.

THE THINGS THAT DISRUPT OUR PEACE

So what is it that disrupts or prevents us from feeling financial peace? The things we bought in the past or buy currently, the hobbies we pick up, the trips we take, the meals out, the gifts we buy, and everything else we buy all have the potential of being influenced by the Joneses. By Joneses, I mean your actual neighbors regardless of their real last names. But, like mentioned in an earlier chapter, I also mean the marketing messages that are flung at us thousands of times a day as well as the social media portrayals of the lives of others.

Each marketing message—the formal ones that come from a company and the informal ones that come via a friend or coworker or your neighbor's lifestyle—can be a little intrusion of discontent into your soul. It can interrupt the serenity you have been enjoying with your life, and introduce the idea that something external might be added to finally make you more happy.

There follows a feeling of restlessness, discontent, and commonly a desire and ability (thanks to credit) to get that thing in your life. Many of my poorest financial decisions, whose effects have stuck around the longest, were made to impress others, not myself or my plans for the future.

The stress of managing those expectations, and the very real repercussions of them (in the form of payments, maintenance, and guilt) can be paralyzing. Can you relate to the stress of having little wiggle room between the payments, bills, and living expenses of your life? The bummer reality is that they have to be paid rain or shine, sick or well, vacationing or working, recession or boom.

This stress further causes tension in relationships, self-loathing, hopelessness, worry about the present, fear of the future. If we could keep financial stress relegated to a single area of our lives, all this money management stuff might be a little more optional. But what you do with your money really governs what kind of life you have, how much peace you enjoy in your relationships, and how prepared you can be for future events.

RECLAIMING YOUR PERSONAL PEACE

When you start doing something about your financial situation, peace becomes an almost immediate companion. It's like a baby fighting sleep. This happens to be one of the great paradoxes of life, that the people who are able to sleep copiously (babies) want it the least, and those who want it the most (adults) typically struggle to get enough.

Anyway, I was saying, oh yes, babies fight the very thing they need. In a similar way, we adults have a profound ability to fight against things like realistic money management that are going to improve our lives radically. But when we finally stop fighting it, stop making excuses for why it doesn't work or why it wouldn't work, stop denying our financial reality, and stop trying to spend like other people, peace distills upon the kingdom.

> "Inner peace begins the moment you choose not to allow another person or event to control your emotions."
>
> Pema Chodron

Even though your *situation* may not be changed overnight, the nagging feeling that all is not well, that you should be more responsible, magically dissipates. It's like a specter that can't live in the light. Peace of mind is a gift that comes to you when you are making a committed effort and looking at all the facts of your situation, denying nothing.

If you're not feeling peace in your finances but claim to be budgeting, I would ask you how honest you are with money. And I would encourage you to change your system. In all my money conversations, I have yet to meet a person who didn't experience lasting change and life-changing peace once they gave up hypothetical budgeting for the type of money management we're talking about in this book.

In contrast, I have had plenty of coaching conversations with plenty of people who have marvelous excuses for why it's best they plug along in the same fashion, getting the same results. Only they can be the judge of how much financial peace they have with their money, but from where I'm sitting, it isn't much.

KEEPING IT SIMPLE

Your life may tangibly be simpler when you start proactively planning your spending. You may eat out less, buy fewer things, take more modest vacations. But not because you have to. You simplify and reduce spending because you choose to, because you want to. Because you wanted something else— either immediate or long-term—more than you wanted the Ruth's Chris dinner.

Joshua Becker is the writer at BecomingMinimalist.com. His first short book, *Simplify: 7 Guiding Principles to Help Anyone Declutter Their Home and Life*, celebrates owning less to enjoy living more. Who hasn't been down the road of a home decor project, or re-doing a room in their house? It sounds fun, which is why we embark in the first place. Sometimes it is something you intrinsically want to do, but often it's influenced by what you see in the homes of others or on social media. You think, if only we had just the right couch for this space, or if all my lighting and hardware matched, or if that wall wasn't there. Or if my decor was a little more...tied together and current.

I'm not downplaying investing in your home, and I'm a big sucker for a cozy space. But from experience, I know how much time these pursuits take, and find myself gaining more satisfaction by crossing projects off my list than in endlessly pursuing just the right look.

A non-tacky, decorative plate in my sister's kitchen says, "Contentment is the greatest treasure." I know this plate well because, well, I gave it to her. These five words speak volumes.

And when you start to plan your money in advance and potentially simplify your spending in order to meet your goals, this peaceful contentment can be yours.

PRACTICAL PEACE

And then there's the peace that comes from being prepared for the unexpected. At the time of writing this, three years have passed since the beginning of the Coronavirus pandemic. Speaking of that chapter: In Utah where I lived at the time, we also had the biggest earthquake the state had seen in decades— just one month into the pandemic.

That earthquake, coincidentally, happened the morning I decided to pull myself out of the pandemic slump and start embracing healthy habits. You know, habits like getting up at a decent hour, getting ready for the day at the start of the day, and eating food that didn't contain massive quantities of preservatives. I was thus in the shower when the earthquake hit, and for weeks afterward, my showers were *much* shorter. I didn't want to be caught in that vulnerable situation in case something bigger hit.

Elsewhere in the country and world, we read or hear about tornadoes and other devastating storms. Unemployment soared from 4.4% in March 2020 to 14.7% in April 2020[20] and as of May 2023, tech companies have laid-off 187,000 employees.[21] Conflict abounds throughout the world, including the invasion of Ukraine by Russia beginning in February 2022. Thankfully, some financial effects of the pandemic have been mitigated somewhat, but new ones have certainly cropped up: inflation, anyone? If anyone needed reminders that the future has and will always be uncertain, we have had them in spades recently.

To meet a constellation of events like this with no savings and lots of debt would be incredibly stressful. Had the perfect storm of 2020 hit in 2013 instead, I would have been paralyzed by fear of losing my job and not being able to make ends meet. And while I can't say I didn't experience any stress, I was able to meet the 2020 pandemic with a robust emergency fund, some emergency supplies, and, most importantly, an organized money system that allowed me to feel some semblance of control. I had some space, so to speak, between me and the cliff of uncertainty.

If you have figuratively been camping right on the edge of the cliff and living paycheck to paycheck, resolve that you never again will. The peace you can have even in the face of uncertainty is worth every ounce of effort invested in changing your habits. It's worth dropping any excuses you've been making. It's worth making an honest assessment; and is way better to do that now than when the uncertain future rears its head.

There is no way to be protected completely from tragedy in life, but to have some amount of financial buffer between you and job loss is certainly freedom from disturbance. To have some reserves of cash is a buffer between you and even the lesser things that break and cost money to fix—cars, water heaters, an ankle. And knowing that you have the ability to manage resources proactively instead of reactively gives you a practical system that will support you in times of plenty as well as times of lean.

Think of the story from the Bible of Joseph in Egypt. Thanks to Pharaoh's dream and Joseph's interpretation of it, the Egyptians were able to prepare for seven years for the next seven years of famine. Others, including Joseph's own family, came to Egypt for relief during the years of famine since they were not prepared. The fact that Egypt could survive those years of hunger and leanness teaches an invaluable lesson about the practical benefits of living wisely now and preparing for a rainy day. I know which side of the dynamic I would prefer to be on.

All this said, the peace you will feel is not so much correlated to the dollars in your emergency fund but rather to the fact that you did *something* to prepare. That you were at least on a path of responsibility for yourself and your family. That you had reversed course from one of financial lack of awareness and irresponsibility to one of empowerment and intention. And this new course is one you can maintain—peacefully—whatever comes.

Chapter 11

LIFE CLARITY

E ach of the benefits talked about in this book are, in and of themselves, profound and life-changing. But speaking of life, let's talk about one final "best thing" about organizing your money, one thing that is super relevant to the life you'll lead and the legacy you'll leave.

The method of planning and organizing your money described in this book can't help but bring you face to face with the life you're creating. Perhaps this is one reason many people avoid budgeting. You may not like what your poor money management says about you, or what your spending habits say about your priorities. Joe Biden, quoting his father, said "Don't tell me what you value, show me your budget, and I'll tell you what you value.[22]

THE POWER OF WHY

Like we've talked about earlier in the book, it is an eye-opening experience to confront your actual financial reality. Not the version of it you've been carefully curating. The version where you admit to yourself what you spend money on before you spend it. It no longer works to say, "I never spend money on clothes," since you'll have to cover those purchases from somewhere when you are actually managing your money.

When you really start forecasting and budgeting as described in this book, you get a clear sense of the priorities in and substance of your life. They may not be intentional, and the longer you've not been proactively planning your money, the more likely it is that your money is spending itself.

Is your life made up of debt-funded or boredom-funded things you don't actually enjoy that much or even remember? Convenience food, drinks, great quantities of cheap—or expensive—clothing, expensive dinners at restaurants someone else picked, home decor you liked for a couple weeks?

Is your life made up of excuses for why your financial and life situation is not your fault?

Are you convinced, despite so much evidence to the contrary, that more money and preferably massive amounts of it, is the only way you are going to be able to get ahead and live the life of your dreams?

When you budget for long enough, it will eventually lead you to answer clarifying questions, like, "Why am I doing _____?" and, "Why do I spend like I do?" And then you get to ask yourself whether you like your answers to these questions. Whether you like where your approach will lead or what options you will not have if you continue to spend like you are. Or whether you even like the stuff of your life.

WHAT IS ACTUALLY IMPORTANT TO YOU?

With this life audit, you really do come face to face with what's important to you. Based on where you put your dollars, is it more important to get your expensive daily drinks than that you become debt-free?

Is it more important to furnish your home like everyone else on the block than to have a home that represents you and your simple tastes?

Is it more important to you that you keep up with every fashion trend than that you save up for the business you say you want to start? (That's definitely been a chapter in my life story.)

When you start putting numbers on some of your unwillingly and previously hidden-in-the-weeds habits, spending behaviors, and price tags on your purchases and priorities, you may find quite a discrepancy between the actual spending and your core principles. And knowing that this exists is powerful. Because once you know it, you can do something about it instead of just perpetuating it.

When you take the reins and finally become the proactive boss of your money, you get a sense for what is possible immediately, as well as what your legacy can be *if* you change your attitudes and habits around money.

When you spend money willy-nilly and without a plan, you never really know if you're trading your time and resources for things of substance and things that you really want beyond today. But when you get on purpose with your money, you start to know what *you* really enjoy, what things are "worth it" to you.

> Once everything is brought into the open and planned for, you get to get on purpose with your money and your life.

Whether you aspire to great wealth or not, much can be learned from some of the wealthiest investors. Instead of traveling by private jet, Sir John Templeton preferred coach, saying "I've got a lot better ways to spend my money than to waste it by getting a bigger seat."[23] Another of the super-rich, Tom Gayner, "Can't bear to buy food in airports and can barely bring himself to pay for two restaurant meals a day while on vacation."[24] And Warren Buffett notoriously enjoys McDonald's most mornings. They have better things to spend their money on. More than that, they have decided there is more to life than spending money, especially on expensive food or material stuff.

I'm reminded of a contrast I witnessed firsthand on a flight re-turning from Lincoln, Nebraska to Las Vegas, where I was living at the time. Most of the occupants of the flight were starting their live-large-Vegas-vacations early, spending ridiculous amounts of money on bagged snacks and overpriced beverages. I'm talking $4 for a snack size bag of chips, y'all. When the flight attendants collected cash for their pick-a-seat lottery game, nearly everyone on the flight paid $5 to get in for the first round, and a surprising number paid the $10 or $20 for Round Two.

As I observed all this, I couldn't help but be struck by the contrast happening across the aisle from me. A couple in their mid-fifties didn't participate in the general frivolity happening around us, but sat quietly reading and talking. And an hour or so after takeoff, they pulled out an obviously homemade but well-made lunch. Thirteen years later, it still stands out as a quiet but profound lesson for not getting swept up in what the crowd is doing—in spending like the crowd is spending.

Once you see where your spending is out of alignment with your values, making changes won't feel like drudgery. For the first time, you will *want* to make adjustments to how you prioritize your buying and spending. For example, if you're eating out at expensive restaurants out of habit—but what you really want to be pursuing is debt freedom—you'll intentionally start allocat-ing fewer dollars to eating out. If you would rather buy a house than go on every vacation family and friends suggest, you'll start graciously saying no and squirrel away the dollars you would have spent. You'll start spending to make your big dreams come true instead of maintaining a status quo you actually don't care to maintain.

THE OPPORTUNITY

I'm no gardener, but I do know that for bushes and fruit trees to thrive, they require pruning. Someone who cares about the yield and health of that tree comes in with pruning shears and lops off the unnecessary or unhealthy branches. They assess and trim, always with an eye toward the health of the plant and facilitating its natural shape and growth. Downward branches are removed, some branches are trimmed to prevent disease, and others are pruned to facilitate blooming.

Can you see how similar this process is to assessing your spending habits and planning your money differently? These "nips and tucks" on the tree means the tree as a whole can grow strong and healthy as opposed to withering fruitlessly and prematurely.

If you never organize or plan your money, you will never have a chance to identify unnecessary or unfruitful spending habits. No matter how much money you make or spend, you may realize that you are spending so much more than you ever intended on gas station snacks and drinks. Figuratively or literally.

Spending categories have wandered into your life and grown much bigger than you realized, and certainly bigger than you ever intended. Even if you have been technically affording these expenses, you didn't realize how big that category had grown or just how many other things you'd rather do with that money.

You realize this only when you come face to face with all your current spending habits. You realize what spending is not actually important to you and what spending really is. And it's amazing how much easier it is to make choices, like remove or trim certain expenses you won't even miss, when you're proactive about organizing your money.

What you worried would feel like deprivation instead feels like a relief. It's like a fairy godmother (your potential, best self) has swept into your disorganized home and helps you get everything shipshape in preparation for the move you've been wanting to make. She sits down with you and helps you pack up the important and necessary things, declutters and fills bags and bags with stuff that does not need to make the journey to your dream home.

You've got awesome things to be doing, but you've been spending like your best plan was to end up in a figurative shack eating cheap Ding Dongs. You've got a way brighter future than this; once you've audited your current life against this bright future and your values, you can spend like it.

A PAUSE

For years and until only recently, I received a newsletter each month. In the mail. Yes, in this online era, someone is still writing, printing, and mailing an old-fashioned newsletter, and I really like it! Sometimes there are interesting discounts on car services, but I mostly open it because it's like a miniature Reader's Digest in that it contains quotes, trivia, recipes, and motivational blurbs. In a day and age of mostly digital content, it's fun to have something tangible to skim. One of my favorite quotes in the February 2017 edition was:

> "The cheaper you can live, the greater your options."
>
> Mark Cuban

All that lead-up for a short quote, I know. It's not particularly eloquent and won't go down in the wisdom of the ages, but the principle is timeless. During my debt-payoff sprint, I was, by choice, focused on my version of living cheap so I could get out of debt. Lest you think of me as a martyr, it honestly wasn't *that* cheap. I was just so much more intentional about my money than I'd ever been before, and therefore life was less expensive.

For years, and well before I embarked on my new money chapter, I had become interested in reducing the amount of "stuff" (i.e. material possessions) in my life. The combination of these two focuses has been life-changing. I have much more of a handle on my consumer spending and habits. I see more clearly what I value and what I want to afford and bring into my life. You could say that I became more intentional about a lot of life. The commitments I said yes to, my possessions and what I chose to keep, and how I planned and organized my money.

Along the way, I have been awakened to a few things:

1. The goal of living on a budget or living cheaply is *not* to be permanently satisfied living cheaply or to become stingy or obsessed with money. I picture Scrooge McDuck in early cartoons counting gold coins in a treasure chest in a sparsely-furnished room. Not the goal. Sometimes it is necessary given temporary financial circumstances, but it is never the long-term goal to be satisfied with barely getting by.

2. We each have unrealized potential that we've not yet begun to realize. We are on the earth to do good with our talents and means and enjoy much.

3. We are meant to aim for a purpose. We know this because we are happiest when striving toward and achieving something bigger than just daily survival.

4. We maximize our individual potential when we wake up to our actual circumstances, make adjustments to our habits, and get in charge of what has previously been a reactionary approach to money.

You can spot purpose in the way some people go about life. You can hear in their voice that they are headed somewhere. They approach decisions and choices intentionally, always influenced by their values and purpose.

As described in an earlier chapter on progress, something magical happens when a person, aimlessly drifting in a boat on a lake (you're welcome for another of my mental images) picks a point on the shore to aim for and starts making headway toward it. If obstacles get in the way, he finds a way around them. If waves come up and toss him about a lil' bit, he'll fight to get back on course. And eventually, he makes it.

Having my sights set on getting out of debt—and importantly, having a timeline for it—was life-changing. Of course I had a few hiccups along the way, but the results of my new budgeting system and approach to money were so apparent and awesome that I always got back on track. Unlike other chapters and years of my life, I never lost visual contact with my target on the shore.

After becoming debt-free and saving gobs of money beyond that point, I am on a different lake, so to speak, working toward other targets on the shore. But the budgeting system and approach to planning my spending and organizing my money is very much the same.

You know how Mark Cuban tells us we'll have more options if we live cheap? Well, it certainly proved true for me. I chose to spend more intentionally and make some spending adjustments in order to become debt-free. And when I was free from massive monthly debt payments, I had a lot more "shore" to choose from and consider than when I was shackled with consumer debt.

What's your vision? What are some of your life's purposes? What do you think you uniquely are here to contribute? What would you do (for work, with your time) if you didn't need the money? Most people never have the chance to find out, but I sincerely hope you do. I hope you choose to get there.

There are things in this world that can only be done by you. And when you are not perpetually strapped for cash, or stressed about money, or ashamed of your past decisions, you'll be more at liberty (figuratively and literally) to accomplish them and realize your potential.

PART 3: THE HOW

Getting excited about a better approach to money is more than half the battle. Believing that there *is* a way that works, and that you can be different with money is the hardest part of the financial change of heart that leads to lasting change.

If I've done my job in the book thus far, you can wonderfully see how this kind of money management, including budgeting, has only upsides. The final part of this book is dedicated to showing you *how* to make this possible for yourself.

In it, I'll share with you the steps that I used to pay off my debt and change my life. These steps apply to all kinds of income scenarios, even those of you who are self-employed or who make variable income. Clients of all income levels have used these same high-level steps to break up with debt, gain traction, enjoy their spending more, sleep better at night, and afford things they formerly thought were out of reach.

And they can work for you, too. For those who feel any lingering dread over the actual *doing*, you will likely benefit from letting someone you trust into your money life—a therapist, a financial coach, a trusted mentor. It can be incredibly healing to let someone else *hear* and *help* with the money thoughts you've been carrying for a really long time now, especially because those ones tend to be shame- and stress-filled.

When you're ready to dive into the doing, each of the following chapters is dedicated to one particular step. They are provided here in summary fashion so you can see where we're heading:

- Step 1: Identify your why

- Step 2: Get everything on paper

- Step 3: Get your "magic number"

- Step 4: Map out your journey

- Step 5: Set up a budget system

- Step 6: Budget current money

- Step 7: Use your budgeting system

Let's dive into the doing, shall we?

Chapter 12

IDENTIFY WHAT YOU WANT

> "He who has a why to live for can bear almost any how."
>
> Friedrich Nietzsche

This famous quote is attributable to Friedrich Nietzsche and often quoted by Viktor Frankl who saw the principle play out in Nazi concentration camps. He saw that those who had something "pulling them ahead" in life were most likely to survive their sufferings.

What is it you really want? What are you aiming toward? No one manages and budgets their money just because it's "fun" and they're looking for a good time. You manage money so that your life dreams can come true. But if you don't have a good idea of what you want, your motivation to manage money consistently will be low.

What do you want to do, be, have, see, contribute? Pay off debt? Buy a house? Stop living paycheck to paycheck? Build a reserve of several months' living expenses? Pay cash for your next car? Be able to eat out more or afford higher-quality groceries for eating at home?

Get more education? Buy a horse ranch? Own land? Travel the world for a year? Volunteer for a year in a refugee camp? Open a quilting/pie/advice shop? Pursue professional figure skater status as an adult just learning to ice skate?

Why do you want it, and why now? What is it about that thing that you want so badly? Why is now—not two years ago, and not five years into the future—the exact right time to start being different with money to make these viable options in the near future?

Do you want your money to be different so that you: Are not continually stressed about money? Finally feel like a real adult with money? Never again have the embarrassment of overdrawing your checking account? Get the "raise" you'll get when you get to keep all the money formerly going to debt? Have options for how and where you live and work? Can live life more on your terms and less on the terms of others? Can contribute in the unique ways that having (even a little extra) money allows?

Note that anything beginning with "should" is not a great reason for why you want your money to be different. You may believe, like I do, that we are stewards of what God gives us, and a sincere desire to be wise with it can motivate better management. But this is very different from a guilt-driven "should," which won't last very long as a reason why you are changing your relationship with money. You'll resent the process, and you'll resent yourself for signing up for it.

Your "why" becomes a powerful shield between you and your previous patterns and the source of the motivation you'll need to continue. But maybe you don't have a super compelling why. Or it all feels too impossible to even consider, and you're figuratively staring at me blankly with shoulders raised in a hopeless shrug. Let's talk about it, shall we?

Here's a wild thought: What if your "why" hasn't come to you yet because you're hopeless about or feel like a mess with money? And that your "why" will bubble to the top as soon as you approach money like it matters what you do with it.

It's like there are amazing things in the wings just waiting for you to get on purpose with your money. How's that for some cool reframing?

WHAT ARE YOU WAITING FOR?

Mel Robbins has become one of my favorite influencers after I came across her book *The 5 Second Rule* several years ago. No, this is not an exposé on eating things off the floor within five seconds, but rather, a book about simply taking action, and quickly. One of her oft-asked questions is, "What are you waiting for, to do _____?" You get to fill in the blank.

I don't know about you, but I have a laundry list of things that could fill in that blank. I have a product that would be perfect for QVC and every household, two app ideas, skills I want to learn, books I want to write, places I want to travel, service I want to render, that land I want to buy in Montana, and additional businesses I want to start. That's just to name a few. I'm sure you have tons of exciting things that could fill in that blank. Some might overlap with mine, but others are uniquely yours.

Basically, we all have cool stuff we want to do. Stuff that will bring joy and satisfaction and accomplishment to your life, help the society of which we are all part, and hopefully make a difference to individuals in it.

Did you know Winston Churchill wrote prolifically in addition to being the British Prime Minister during one of the trickiest times in the world's history? He literally wrote dozens of books. And I think we can all imagine how little spare time he had. #noexcuses.

For those without a clearly defined reason why you need to change your money situation, let's have a quick chat about that. There may be circumstances necessitating a change in your money habits, but until you have a "why" that you really want, it won't fuel you much.

To dig deeper, I'd recommend you look more closely at the things you have crossed off your What's Possible In Life list. What are some big things you dreamed about—things you wanted to have, places you wanted to live or travel, causes you wanted to influence? Start entertaining the thought that at least some of these might actually be possible.

One reason you might be waiting to start your things and sign up for a "why" might be your money situation. But isn't it crazy how long you have let that be a showstopper? Like years? You are doubly waiting; waiting to start changing your money situation so that you can start the other big thing(s).

What are you waiting for financially? Are you waiting to get more money? Are you waiting for a new month or new year in order to start? Are you waiting for a reason to get your finances in order? Are you waiting for budgeting to not involve any thought or energy? I know I did all the above! But there are loads of people who had less than ideal circumstances (financial and otherwise) and still did incredible things.

Regardless of what you have been waiting for, the good news is that you can start changing it today! Literally. You can say—today—that you are going to do things differently and make actionable steps to change your finances or reach your goals. You can recognize the pointlessness of waiting for the world to beg you to chase your dream. Sometimes that would be really nice, but it's probably not going to happen. Starting might feel scary, but starting the thing, doing the thing, is so much scarier from the sidelines than in the actual arena.

Years ago, I played indoor soccer for a glorious three weeks. The co-ed team was desperate for women and this is why they invited the girl who had literally never played any version of organized soccer. Standing on the sidelines, I was terrified. But once I was pulled in, my condition was downgraded from "terrified" to just "scared" and eventually "excited" because I was now *doing* the thing.

THE POWER IN TAKING ACTION

Just start. Scared or not, send the email, make the phone call, sign up for the thing. Start the budget. Start outlining the book. Confront the facts you've been afraid to acknowledge. These are tangible actions that commit us to a course of action and, regardless of the outcome, progression. You've ventured. You've dared. And yes, sometimes the part of you that craves security and comfort might regret it.

But the part of you that knows you are here on Earth to grow will be just pleased as punch.

> "The world rewards those of us who are coura-
> geous enough to stop waiting and start."
>
> Mel Robbins

This is the rationale behind some gutsy messages I send these days. As my finger hovers over the send button, my mind races with all the ideas why I shouldn't send it, or why they won't say yes, or why I'm not ready. But I haven't regretted any of them.

I'm surprised by the number of "yes" responses I have received. And even when I don't receive huge "yes" responses, I can tell you that it feels so empowering to just do. Like runners at the start of a race, there is a moment when the gun goes off. And they start running. Too often we are like a runner who spends hours perfecting their position at the starting line but who never actually runs. Give yourself the starting signal and just go!

The solution is almost always found in action. I have a problem that I'm sure no one else experiences (insert sarcasm), and that is being unsure of which of my projects to work on. This usually leads to a downward spiral of no motivation.

> In the Land of No Motivation, it's easy to think the solution is to be found in the arrival of motivation. But nope. The solution is always found in action.

Pretty much any positive action will do. It's like the action—whether it be relevant to the task list you're avoiding or just calling a friend or doing some service—nudges us back to the purposeful path we are on. Inaction pulls us off the path and toward the sirens of self-doubt, laziness, and selfishness, and the quickest way back to the path forward is action.

So, pal, what fills in the blank for you? What are the cool things you want to do? By cool, I mean rewarding, fruitful, difference-making, and the like. What are you waiting for? And most importantly, what are you going to do—today—to start?

Chapter 13

GET EVERYTHING ON PAPER

With clear reasons to do money differently, let's dive into your current money situation. One of my favorite mantras is, "Deal with real." What do I mean by this?

I mean surfacing all the fixed, practical expenses of your life calmly and rationally on paper or, preferably, a spreadsheet. And after reading this chapter, I dare you to do it! No more avoiding looking under the bed, afraid of what you might find there.

It hasn't served you to pretend like your life costs less than it does, and yet, it is the path of least resistance so it's easy to do.

I really like the book *Great Expectations*. I'll do a really poor job of summarizing it, but here's the gist:

Pip is poor.

Pip comes into money.

Pip spends his money extravagantly because that's what he thinks he's supposed to do.

Pip and his buddy have cheerful "financial-reckonings" where they review the dismal gap between their income and expenses, resolve to change, but don't.

Pip loses all his money, starts over at the bottom and finally and successfully makes his way in the world.

If there are any other notable classics you'd like me to similarly slaughter, please let me know. Anyway, the point of this story is that, as bleak as Pip's circumstances were, he gained at least some peace and clarity by getting the facts and figures down on paper.

FIXED EXPENSES

These are the "bill" expenses that currently happen monthly or annually at a relatively fixed amount.

Note: This category of expense does not include things like Groceries, since this will be covered in the next section when we talk about flexible spending. Groceries and a lot of other things fit appropriately under the flexible spending category since you could technically spend nothing on Groceries by eating out of your pantry or awkwardly soliciting invitations to meals.

List monthly expenses and annual expenses (broken down into a monthly cost). Including annual costs in your monthly cost of living makes them much more real and much less of a surprise when they happen. It's incredibly useful to see what your average monthly cash flow is so you can see what can realistically be saved or used for debt payments.

Remember Jill, who I mentioned in an earlier chapter? The one who wanted to skip ahead to creating a budget that she could finally love? Getting everything on paper was the ticket—when she was ready for it—to an approach to money that can last. You get really important information out of this exercise, and it answers a lot of questions about why you've felt stressed.

Some fixed expenses are obvious and easily accounted for. Others are easier to forget about and have a sneaky way of accumulating. Review this list of common fixed expenses—the bills that you're committed to for a recurring amount until you change the arrangement—and list out all the expenses that apply to you. Be sure to add any that apply to your unique situation that are not listed here.

- Mortgage or rent

- Utilities: Internet, cable, trash & water, sewer, HOA, electric, gas

- Memberships (both monthly and annual): Gym, Netflix, Amazon Prime, Audible, other streaming services

- Car expenses: Tires, registration, insurance, repairs, car payment

- Medical expenses: Office visit copays, dentist/orthodontist costs

- Minimum debt payments: Credit card payments, student loans, personal loan payments

- Family expenses: Daycare, enrollment fees, tuition

- Pet expenses: Boarding, pet insurance, grooming

Be thorough! Part of the problem of the past has been underestimating how expensive life is. This exercise—if done thoroughly—can prevent the vast majority of financial surprises. The price of not accepting all the realities of your current financial situation is guilt and stress that you just can't seem to make ends meet.

FLEXIBLE SPENDING

Now that you have all the fixed expenses down on paper, let's move into flexible spending. Continued honesty as you move into this category of spending is critical. Most of us greatly underestimate our flexible spending, and this is what leads to lots of unhealthy credit card spending.

Especially when things are tight, it can be hard to acknowledge even to yourself that you actually do things like buy clothes and eat out. Or that you spend more on these categories and others than you want to admit.

I know from plenty of experience; not only was I not acknowledging that my shopping splurges happened, but I certainly was not acknowledging that they cost me hundreds if not thousands of dollars per year.

So today we sweep the rest of everything into the center of the room. When everything's out in the open, you can finally begin to make sense of your financial picture. You can make decisions that you can't when things are hiding in corners.

Write down all other spending in the categories with wiggle room.

- Groceries and Take-out

- Entertainment: Concerts, movies, hobbies

- Eating out: Family dining out, personal dining out

- Kid expenses: Allowance, birthday parties, sports/music/ dance costs, clothes, haircuts

- Your expenses: Haircuts/colors, clothes, makeup, personal enrichment

- Gifts: Christmas, baby/bridal showers, gifts for friends at work, etc.

- Target: This is not a real category, but I include it as a sample of a spending black hole that might need to be untangled for you to make sense of that spending.

- Household: Cleaning supplies, toiletries, postage/shipping Home improvement/decorating

- Gas for the car

- Donations

Before you wrap up this step, ask yourself, "What else?" Then ask it again and again and again, thinking of both monthly and annual expenses. Feel free to review your credit card or checking account to further jog your memory. There are major rewards for honesty at this step. Surfacing *all* your numbers to the light of day allows you to make much better decisions with and about them.

Advice: Be realistic with your amounts. Deal with what is real *right now,* and doIt was gratifying and helpful to help a client I'll call Jan with this very thing. She and her husband were in the second half of life, newly married, and had created a budget together. She was coming to me for help sticking to their budget since she assumed it was due to overspending that they weren't able to save $1,500 per month as planned. In actuality, it was the case that their life cost about $1,200 per month more than they appreciated when they created the budget.

They'd listed out the fixed (bill) expenses and the things their household was on the hook for each month. They'd also estimated amounts for things like food, entertainment, gifts and trips.

Given the amounts they'd surfaced, and given their sizable income, it seemed obvious to them both that there would easily be $1,500 left for saving every month. The problem was a Miscellaneous category. Like the junk drawer every house has, this was a category created to cover all the other stuff that hadn't bubbled up elsewhere in their budget.

$500 seemed like it should be ample to cover all the miscellaneous stuff. However, when she and I examined all their miscellaneous spending, they needed more like $1,000 in this category. Additionally, as we did the exercise of reviewing *all* their current flexible spending, it became evident that their approximations for many categories were much lower than reality.

The combination of lower-than-reality projections and unsurfaced, miscellaneous expenses are a major contributor to the stress you feel around money. It's only in getting what you really spend down on paper that you can make decisions about adjusting spending, then budget and stick with it. Otherwise, you will do what I did for years: lament that the "budget" isn't working, blame yourself, and feel like you just cannot seem to get ahead. But here's the thing: It is really, really hard to exert discipline to keep something organized when you don't have an accurate picture of what is happening.

Chapter 14

SEE YOUR "MAGIC" NUMBERS

Once you have surfaced all possible expenses, you're going to face your moment of glorious truth. This is a powerful moment that really matters. Because today you find out if you are actually living within your income or beyond it.

And while it seems like only one of those outcomes is exciting, I would argue that both are. As long as it remains a closely guarded secret—even, or especially, from yourself—that you're overspending, you're living in denial and likely beating yourself up for spending too much or being bad with money. But once you find that you are definitely spending more than you make, at least that fact is out in the open.

And when something is in the open versus obscured in the dark, you can decide what to do about it.

WHAT IS YOUR MONTHLY BUFFER?

To get your monthly buffer, simply subtract your now-fully-surfaced monthly spending from your monthly income.

Remember, your monthly spending should include annual expenses broken down into monthly amounts. You've been dealing with ballpark numbers for so long and are now dealing with reality. It's empowering to know that this buffer number is one you can now plan with, since it's not a loosey-goosey made-up figure.

This number allows you to finally make realistic plans and projections for your future, something you've not been able to do for some time or ever. Even if you've previously used spreadsheets and debt-payoff calculators, if you've not been thorough and honest about the inputs, it's been impossible to plan for the outputs and get results you want.

DO YOU WANT TO MAKE ANY CHANGES?

Now you get to ask yourself, what do I want to do about this number?

If it's zero or positive:

If there is no gap at all between your income and realistic cost of living, it's worth celebrating that you are breaking even. And you have a ton of company, given that 60% of U.S. consumers were living paycheck to paycheck as of August 2022.[25]

If it's positive, awesome! You get to make some cool decisions with that. Whether you have a $15 buffer or a $1,500 buffer, now's your moment to appreciate that you are in the positive and can likely exercise some choice to become *even more* cashflow positive.

You do not have to keep your $100 cable bill, or keep leasing a car for $550 per month, or keep giving extravagant gifts to everyone you know. You may *choose* to keep these expenses in your life, but this is wildly different than passively letting them simply stick around without you choosing them.

If it's negative:

If your magic number is negative (you spend more than you make), this is the time to change that number. Too many people never even arrive at this decision point because they never surface how much life costs them. You, though, have, and the same beautiful gift of choice is yours. What are you going to do to change it? Your options include increasing your income or trimming expenses, or a combination of both. This is easier said than done in some situations and I am for sure not disregarding or undermining the potentially stressful situation you're in.

That said, I have witnessed clients make significant positive changes when they've embraced their *full* financial reality. Armed with facts, I've seen multiple clients quickly find ways to increase their income or trim spending in ways that didn't qualitatively affect their quality of life.

My gentle reminder is that failing to correct a negative monthly cashflow situation will—at some point—have a discouraging impact on your overall financial prospects and limit your options. And I don't want that for you.

The only way for you to live on more than you make is to fund the difference with credit cards or loans. And to do so either monthly or sporadically when occasional and annual expenses come up that you have not worked into your monthly plan. Either way, you will see a mounting debt balance for you to confront at some point. You also experience daily, weekly, and monthly stress as you try to make ends meet. Sleep gets compromised. Your ability to focus at work is diminished. At some point, you have to say "no" to necessities if your credit is maxed. And guess how many of your dreams you'll have the money or energy for chasing?

Can you tell that I'd strongly encourage you to deal with overspending as it happens instead of using debt to cover it? I speak from lots of stressful experience.

THE OTHER EXCITING NUMBER

If you are currently making monthly debt payments, it's important to get excited about getting out of debt. Determine how much of your current money is not available to you because it's claimed for monthly debt payments. It was very motivating to become debt-free when I realized that over $1,000 was being figuratively garnished for debt payments every single month. How much will you get to keep every single month when your debt is paid off?

And what will you do, or be able to do, with that amount of money each month? Journal about it, in gorgeous, creative detail.

Chapter 15

CREATE YOUR MAP

N ow that you have an accurate picture of your spending, and assuming you've got some wiggle room or
made some adjustments to give yourself some wiggle room
in your monthly picture, you're going to use that number to
create a map for yourself.

You'll use your positive buffer number, however small, to
map out your path to whatever other financial goal you have.
Your action for this chapter is to, on paper, map out how
much progress you will have made and what your balance will
be at mileposts along the way.

IF YOUR GOAL IS DEBT-FREEDOM

Which debt are you going to tackle first? Deciding that is a critical
first step. Two popular approaches are to 1) pay off the debt with
the largest balance or highest interest rate or 2) pay off your debts

smallest to largest, starting with the smallest balance. I chose the latter option as I wanted to taste success sooner rather than later.

If you opt to focus on the one with the biggest balance, you'll want to create your own milestones or increments at which you can celebrate. If you choose to "snowball" your debt pay-off and tackle them smallest to largest, you've got built-in milestones. But no matter which option you choose, write out your milestones.

If you pay $____ /month toward the smallest debt while only paying minimum payments on others, when will that smallest debt be fully paid?

And if you add that payment to your next smallest debt, when will that one be paid off? And so on.

Remember story problems from grade school math? Let's go back to that territory, shall we, and play with an oversimplified example.

Let's pretend it's January. 1 You have two credit card balances you want to pay off.

Credit Card #1 has a balance of $500.

Credit Card #2 has a balance of $1,500.

If you pay minimum payments of $75 on Card #2 (not your priority right now), and pay $100/mo toward Card #1 (your current priority), you will have it paid off in five months..

Then, you add the $100 payment you were paying for Card #1 to your monthly payment of Card #2. That balance has been reduced by the minimum monthly payments and let's say it's now $1,200. You are now able to pay $175 toward it, which means you will have it paid off in December.

Seeing the specific months in which debts will be paid off is very motivating, especially because it gives you reason to stay on target or even beat your own goal.

I'm aware that this is a simple example, using small balances and excluding interest. But can you see how the principle works, and how you would continue this with additional debts? And can you critically see how you would gain *momentum*?

It was game-changing for me to see a map with checkpoints to have my debt all the way paid off. It took a big, scary amount of money and broke it into achievable chunks with lots of emotional validation along the way.

You may protest and holler at me: "But wait! Interest will accumulate along a debt payoff journey and that sounds like a lot of hard math to figure out!" True, true, little cricket.

However, I find that it's not helpful to get too in-the-weeds about estimating decreasing monthly payments including the interest. Way more than niggling with complicated maths, you need a plan and a target completion date to work toward and this gives you exactly that.

IF YOUR GOAL IS SAVINGS:

If you're not in debt and your goal is a savings goal: Map out when you'll hit key milestones by saving your above-determined magic number. Maybe it's saving for a down payment on a home, or paying cash for a replacement car, or taking your family on a cash-flowed vacation.

You'll once again list out the months, how much you will add to your goal that month, and what your total balance will be in that month. And while there is not a "savings snowball" effect (since you're not freeing up money like when you pay off a debt), you still give yourself a checkpoint to compare your progress to.

SEEING THE BIG PICTURE

It can be easy to not make the monthly goal, but when you see that doing so affects your whole plan for reaching your goal, it's less attractive to deviate. And, having the months and amounts mapped out has the additional benefit of gamifying your goal; it is a total hit of dopamine when you are able to pay more than planned toward debt or save even more than you planned in a month. This usually happens through unexpected income or by choosing to spend less than budgeted because you wanted to.

Whatever your goal, you can trust this map because you've been honest and thorough in surfacing your numbers. The map has an additional benefit of motivating you, when you see that you are on track at the little check-ins along the way. Even more motivating is when you are able to squirrel away extra toward your goal, and you find that you are ahead of pace. It almost turns into a game, one with amazing and very real-life benefits.

If you remember from back in the beginning of the book, there was a little part where I mentioned inviting my sister over for a Finance Review Party. Yes, I sure know how to throw a party. Anyway, before going on to the next step, I would like to pause for a public service announcement and suggest that right now would be a great time to invite someone to review your numbers and plan.

There's something about being willing to let someone else see your dirty laundry that makes you realize it's not all that dirty.

The poet John Milton said, "Where shame is, there is also fear." If you confront the shame by sharing your real, authentic situation with someone you trust to listen with empathy and not judgment, you'll find a huge weight being lifted off your shoulders.

> The thing you have been so afraid of—others finding out that you have a financial mess— wasn't worth being afraid of after all.

Chapter 16

CREATE YOUR SYSTEM

Pretend something with me for a minute. Imagine being told on arrival to Disneyland that you will be the only adult chaperoning a class of 2nd-graders. There you are, the only adult chaperone, trying to keep track of twenty-five children. In the middle of the mayhem of the Happiest Place on Earth. With no chance to prepare. How smoothly do you think that would go?

Now imagine that you had some notice about this and you could prepare. You come up with a plan that gives you and the kids the best chance of success; you create a system of organization.

You have them wear garishly colored matching t-shirts.

You carry a ridiculously large flower for them to follow through the park.

You create an itinerary and a buddy system, and pause for frequent regroupings as you navigate through the park.

Your phone number is written on each of their arms in Sharpie marker. Sure, there might be a few hiccups and wanderers during the day, but your chances of keeping track of these kids is so much higher than when you had no opportunity for organization.

I bet you see where I'm going with this. The first scenario—no notice, no plan, just hope for the best—is equivalent to how most people manage their money. They do mental gymnastics trying to keep track of all the spending and bills still needing to be paid and what they think they can afford. It's exhausting, not very fun, and not very effective. By the end of the Disney day, you've lost at least five kids.

In contrast, with the method involving a system of organization, your odds of keeping track of all twenty-five kids is much, much higher and involves much less stress. Keeping track of your money and keeping your money on track is infinitely easier when you have a system for doing so. Having a place to organize your actual, current money, then track your spending against it, is game-changing.

The system works best when you've completed the preceding steps, since, if you plug inaccurate numbers into a system, the system is going to struggle. And then because you don't get happy results, you quit. And, tragically, you blame budgeting and the system, thus denying yourself a system that will actually empower you to get unstuck.

So this step is where the numbers you surfaced—on paper in previous steps—become an official, *living* budget. That paper work you did earlier will serve as the hypothetical basis for your *actual* budget where real money is assigned and spending is tracked. This is where a tool becomes critical.

There is no shortage of systems or tools to choose from— homemade spreadsheets, cash envelopes, Mint, EveryDollar, You Need A Budget (YNAB), PocketGuard, HoneyDue, Fudget, and so many more. Banks like Qube combine budgeting with banking, and most credit cards and bank accounts provide at least some level of reporting on spending.

I use and enjoy YNAB and it has been game-changing for several of my clients. While I use it as the point of reference for a budgeting tool in the remainder of this book, it is entirely possible to succeed with other tools or approaches. But if you've felt out of control with spending in the past and are prone to feeling guilty about spending, I recommend a tool that makes the following possible:

1. It facilitates budgeting real money into specific categories—including the fun ones—before you spend.

2. Your money stays organized in these categories until you spend.

3. It is easy to fix mistakes as they happen, and before your plans can be run off the rails too far.

4. It syncs with your financial institutions but does not do all the work for you.

It is a paradigm shift for most people to realize that budgeting is a very literal process, and it involves money only when you get it or spend it. Yes, there is a hypothetical element of how you think or want a month to go, but a budget itself is a living, breathing system involving current dollars.

If you get paid every other week, you budget that money when you get it, of course taking into consideration upcoming needs and when you'll receive more money.

One of the best parts about zero-based budgeting tools is that when you "put" money in a category, it stays there. It stays there until you spend out of the category or until you pull money out of that category to do something else you've deemed more necessary or important.

This sets you up for success as you can fix mistakes or deal with unexpected emergencies when they inevitably happen, instead of doing major damage control at the end of a month. To budget money in fun categories like Vacation and Personal Enrichment and Clothing, and then have it stay there until you spend it, is incredibly motivating. Your money stays safe from unintentional spending outside *your* plan.

TIPS FOR SETTING UP YOUR BUDGET

- Customize categories to match your life. If using a digital budgeting tool, delete any categories that don't apply to you.

- Organize it in a way that is logical to you. As much as your budgeting tool allows, drag and drop categories until they are organized in a way that makes sense to you. You may put things in order of priority or due date or simply group "like with like" (all the kid categories, etc).

- Get as granular as you need to in category creation, but don't create categories for every single expense—you'll set yourself up for the impossible task of keeping a too-long list organized.

- There is no "right" number of categories you ought to have. If you go too granular you will make this harder than it needs to be. But if you lump too many things together you will lose insight into how much you really spend and need. There is a sweet spot, and I promise you will find yours. A few examples of consolidated categories you might consider:

  ○ Hair & Makeup: haircuts, hair and face products, makeup.

  ○ Memberships: annual

- ○ Memberships: monthly memberships.

- ○ Random & Household: Household cleaning products, feminine products, postage, car washes, parking, etc.

Note: If you are self-employed or have variable income, budgeting is–if possible–even more important and relevant to you than for those with predictable paychecks. We'll talk more about this in the next section.

> NOTE: If you haven't already downloaded it, a PDF checklist is available to help you create and use this kind of system (budget). Head to emilyburnett.me/spender to get it. You may also be interested in the "Making the Most of Payday" PDF cheatsheet, available at the same link.

In case anything about this process feels overwhelming, just remember: it's also been overwhelming without a system. You may want to take a minute and reflect on that. A healthy system makes your life better, not harder—even if it takes a fresh approach and some effort. You're just taking a portion of the time you spend stressing about finances, and re-allocating it to proactive measures that make a powerful, happy difference.

This whole money management thing is about learning to trust yourself and being more intentional and less self-sabotage-y with your spending, not "doing budgeting right." You are doing it "right" if you are planning what to do with your money, less stressed about money, and making headway toward your goals.

Chapter 17

ALLOCATE CURRENT MONEY

With your system created, you now get to finally do what I call "budgeting." Answer the question, "What does this money I have right now need to cover before I get paid again?" Take all the dollars you have in your checking and saving accounts, as well as any stashes of cash, and farm them out into your categories for spending and saving. If you let money accumulate in your Venmo, you may want to transfer it into your checking account and make a habit of doing this when you get Venmo money; it otherwise has a way of totally blurring together purchases and reimbursements.

Money blurred together in a single pot puts all the burden on your brain to remember your purposes for it. Not only is that stressful, but it doesn't work great. No offense to your brain! It's just already got a lot going on and trying to remember how much of your money is available for necessary things versus fun things is an unnecessary game of mental gymnastics.

In your budgeting tool, you'll want to get the dollars "To Be Budgeted" down to $0, thus ensuring that every dollar has a "home" and a plan. And if, as you start farming out money, you start going into the negative, you know you've budgeted more money than you currently have. You simply need to adjust some of the categories where you have already allocated money.

Then, when you get more money, budget again. It's very much like looking down the road and planning for all the things you can see. Well, actually, it's exactly like that.

> Budgeting is something you do any time you get money. It's an ongoing, happy process and very much a continual conversation with your money and your plans.

And thank goodness for that! It's really not that much effort, just something you need to actively participate in. Like life. You get out of it what you put in. It's true for relationships, exercise, work, hobbies.

Why we expect budgeting to be any different is beyond me, but I lived in this alternate financial universe myself into my thirties. Stress was the identifying feature of my financial "system" for that entire decade. I put in effort but I never asked for help and I never got totally honest with myself or walked the steps I've outlined here.

You can start right where you are by planning what your current dollars need to cover before you get more money. If that sounds stressful, remember that you are doing some form of it in your head already. With budgeting, we've gotten very attached to starting on the first of the month, but you don't need to wait until the first of next month, or January 1 of next year, or the first day of next quarter. Paychecks don't all come in on the first of the month, and bills certainly don't. Shifting your mindset to allow for budgeting to be something ongoing will help you out immensely. So seriously, start today.

FLUCTUATING INCOME

While you cannot predict with 100% your income for a month, you now have an accurate picture of how much you realistically *spend* on an average month. And when you do get money, you can budget it toward the highest priority or next-occurring transactions and enjoy the peaceful feeling that at least that or those expenses are covered.

You'll see very clearly how much more money you need to cover upcoming categories. And if you have extra high income months, you can budget the buffer ahead into future months.

Chapter 18

USE AND MAINTAIN YOUR SYSTEM

C ongratulations on setting up a budget you can love using. Now comes the fun part—using it. There will be missteps, but with your money organized in this way, these are simply small deviations on your path. They are easily recovered from, and your overall trajectory remains confidently forward.

Even as an avid budgeter, I occasionally overspend categories. Success is not about being perfect. I learn from where I overspend, and adjust my numbers when I realize I have been unrealistic. Sometimes you don't want to admit right out of the gate that you spend $150/month on hair and makeup and facial products. But you really might, and it's better to admit it so you can start allocating money more realistically.

Budgeting like we've talked about is like giving yourself happy guardrails, so that you can figuratively drive more confidently and quickly down the road. It's *incredibly* empowering to spend without worrying that you're going to go irreconcilably off the edge.

And in case you need a reminder, this budget system is the means by which you keep your money organized as *you* decided it needed to be. It is how you cover all your expenses, afford your monthly wants, *and* make progress toward your goals. This third item is the piece that's been especially missing because of drama surrounding covering the monthly needs and wants.

USING IT IN REAL LIFE

So, you've allocated your current money into your categories. Now you go about your life, and spending according to that plan. If your budget is really reflecting your life, including the fun stuff and your future goals, this plan is one you want to use well.

Before you spend, you'll want to look at your category balance(s) instead of your checking account balance. The latter doesn't know a thing about your plans for life, so it's time for it to stop giving you permission to spend. *You* are now the boss of that permission and have decided to keep those decisions organized in your budget; that's why you quickly reference the budget before you spend.

Once you spend, you'll input your spending, either manually or via automatic sync features of whichever tool you use. When you enter a purchase, most transactions will be really straightforward and affect only one category. A few transactions span multiple categories, but most budgeting tools make it easy to "split" a transaction if you want to.

Let's say you went to Target. You checked your budget so you had a pretty good idea of how much you had to spend on the things you knew you needed and wanted. Entering your spending in your budgeting app looks a little something like this:

Total = $127

About $40 of that was Gifts.

About $50 was Make Home More Awesome.

The rest was Groceries, so $37.

You could enter all that spending as Make Home More Awesome, but you probably don't want to deplete that category faster than necessary. Am I right? You absolutely could though—this is your budget and your life.

Using your budget is how you say hello to guilt-free spending. It's the best feeling to see that you still have money left in those categories after you spend. And that categories like Vacation and Utilities and Savings are unaffected by the spending.

And if you do happen to overspend in a category, you just shift money from another category or two. Easy.

This type of budgeting is—wonderfully—not a set-it-and-forget it situation. No more setting financial goals and then crossing your fingers, hoping you like what you see at the end of the month.

You're going to check in every couple days, especially on the categories you spend from the most and where you are prone to overspend. Because, unlike in the past, you don't just get to over-spend on Groceries and Entertainment and Vacations and then feel guilty at the end of the month. With this type of budgeting, you have the opportunity to clean up messes as they happen.

Remember, you're going to look to your budgeting categories to inform your spending decisions instead of your checking ac-count. Because you want to. Because you have motivating plans for your money and your life, and this whole budget thing is just where you are keeping those plans organized.

It doesn't matter a thing to your Dining Out & Entertainment category if you have $20,000 in your checking and savings ac-counts. What matters is how much money you have planned to spend—guilt-free—right now on Dining Out & Entertainment while the rest of your plan stays right on track.

You'll need to **reconcile your budget**, to make sure it matches what the bank says you really have. They're the source of truth here, so it's important to keep your budget matching your bank.

This type of money management is all about trusting yourself and your numbers. This may all be feeling too good to be true. And after years of not trusting yourself or your numbers, you may have a hard time doing so.

Reconciling is what provides reassurance that you are not budgeting with monopoly money and that you *really* can spend the money as you have planned. You'll do this as frequently as you need to to feel comfortable. I recommend at least once per week, especially at first, or every one to two weeks as you get more comfortable with it. At the very least, be sure to reconcile when you get new money.

And don't quit. That's how you win with all of this.

How long did it take you to get good at parts of your job that you didn't previously know how to do? A few weeks? A few months? This is no different. The only difference is that budgeting benefits every single part of your life. So it's worth doing. It's worth learning. It's worth caring about. And by making it this far, you've proved you do.

CONCLUSION

S haquille O'Neal spent his first $1 million paycheck in a single day.[26] On what? Three Mercedes-Benz cars (one for him, two for his parents), diamond jewelry, new suits, and a high-rise condo. A bank manager instigated a conversation with him the next day, reviewing all of these high-ticket purchases with him. In this conversation, the manager told him that most athletes quickly lose everything they've earned and advised Shaq to get serious about taking care of his money.[27]

Shaq certainly did, but he's one of the lucky professional athletes who took that well-intentioned advice. As reported in an oft-cited Sports Illustrated article:

- "By the time they have been retired for two years, 78% of former NFL players have gone bankrupt or are under financial stress because of joblessness or divorce."

and

- "Within five years of retirement, an estimated 60% of

former NBA players are broke."[28]

Even if the article is dated, figures like these help make the case that more money does not prevent financial stress or solve for a broken system. If more money was the solution to financial stress and woes, professional athletes and A-list celebrities should be set for life based on a single year's earnings. But adding money to a broken or nonexistent system of managing it is a lot like pouring money into a bucket with a hole. This sort of bucket requires a steady addition of water just to remain mostly full.

I love sharing the wonders of budgeting because, no matter how big your figurative bucket is, literally any situation is improved by plugging the holes. It's never too early to start creating happy financial habits, and it's also never too late.

Every single financial situation is improved by the things we've talked about in this book:

- Taking stock of exactly and very realistically where you are.

- Creating a system for organizing your money.

- Planning your spending.

- Mapping your route to what you want in life.

- Simplifying accounts and priorities where you can.

Doing these things brings the life-altering benefits shared in this book and prepares you for the additional money coming into your life. And as you get on-purpose with your money, you can more rapidly get on purpose with your life.

My hope is that you are feeling tangibly more empowered to manage your money to get out of debt, build savings, and create options. I hope that "budgeting" has been positively reframed for you.

Can we agree now that budgeting simply means planning your money so you can live richly, as opposed to something that will ruin all your fun in life? You've hopefully learned that even if you don't currently formally budget, you have still been doing some kind of mental magic so you don't routinely spend all your money on Starbucks, concert tickets, vacations, clothes, and eating out. The result of this type of unplanned money is a lot of stress, and the result of actually and intentionally budgeting is a whole lot of peace and direction.

If you really do take the reins in a new way with your money and don't give in to excuses and complaints and "it's too hard" thinking (it's not!), your life will change. That is a promise. You trade the financial stress and juggling you've been doing for financial empowerment and management.

I like a good self-improvement book as much as the next person, maybe more. I read voraciously and have certainly gotten inspired by some of the trendy books of our time. You know the type of book that has messages like "You can do anything!" Or,

"You just need to put it out into the Universe that you want more money and it will come!" Or, "You can literally manifest your dream job and salary if you just visualize it enough!" Or, "If you believe in yourself hard enough, and do big enough things, the money will follow and you will have peace and security..."

Negative thinking is the path of least resistance, and it's a totally worthwhile thing to switch to more positive thinking. And thinking big and optimistically sure can't hurt. However, I spent so many years waffling between self-doubt and financial stress, and marching into the world with the attitude of attraction. I have solidly come to the conclusion that taking control of what is *already* in your life and getting your roots right is what sets you up to really grow from where you are.

WANTING THE LIFE YOU HAVE:

I started this book talking about the clubhouse I failed to build with my little brother because I squandered my portion of funds. That was a long time ago, and a lot has changed. To highlight just how far I've come, let's talk about the book a friend recently recommended. This book is about how every woman can aspire to wealth, and that one way to get there is to get very clear on all the things you want to own, do, become, and have access to.

What car do you want to drive? What kind of clothes do you want to afford? What kind of vacations do you want to take? What kind of household help do you want to have? The list of categories went on and on. And then you are encouraged to take action on at least one of them, thus giving yourself a taste of what it will be like to be able to afford all those things.

As I thought about what I want, I realized something pretty big. I realized the only material thing I want that I don't have is land (and a cozy house on that land) in Montana. And that's not because I'm just an uber-content person. It's because, as I've gotten on-purpose with my money and adopted a system that facilitates me keeping more of that money, I've been able to comfortably afford my wants while taking care of my needs. And I'm completely confident I'll get my land in Montana.

It's a remarkable feeling to legitimately want most of the life you already have.

And I would not have gotten to such a place if I hadn't gotten on-purpose with my money. This is not shared to brag or flex, but simply to show what's possible when you take control of your current money situation and approach it with intention and purpose.

It can take several weeks for people to get the hang of their money system and to really be humming along. However—and this is an important "however"—you will start to see and feel results *immediately*.

It's a bit like a new exercise routine. If you have external physical goals you are working toward, it will take some time to visually see a difference, but you get the endorphins straight away. From

Day 1 you experience benefits such as sleeping better, having increased energy, and experiencing improved self-esteem.

You also start benefiting immediately as you approach your monthly money with intention. And not just in emotional ways! I kept marveling in my first few months that I was paying more on debt but somehow spending more on fun things. It shouldn't have worked that way and yet it did, and it can for you too.

If you are serious about it, that is. And if you've made it this far in a book about proactive money management and budgeting, I'd wager you are. In fact, I'll bet money that this actually will be the time you change—for good—your money life.

Gone will be the unhealthy "I deserve" self-sabotaging behavior that feels good for all of two minutes.

You start wanting an organized and balanced money life more than a Target shopping spree, because you see very clearly that money for that spree has to come out of one of your other categories. And you know that you set money aside in categories for specific purposes, including for your big dreams.

You won't be perfect, and that's okay! No longer will a misstep or a hiccup be a "throw your hands in the air I quit" moment. It will just be a little swerve in the road.

You will go into former overspending situations with a plan. Going out to dinner with friends who like to order generously, then split the bill? What's *your* plan for your money in this situation?

You will experience over and over the reassurance of having money set aside for emergencies like car repairs. You experience this before the emergency, and when it happens.

You will experience the double-dopamine hit of setting money aside for fun things like clothes and vacations. You will feel a thrill knowing that it's there for guilt-free spending and again when you get to do that guilt-free spending.

You will see yourself making marked and lasting progress toward financial freedom. Even if you still have debt while you work your plan, credit is not running the show anymore. You are.

You've got a wonderful present and future on the line. Don't let your money spend it. Be the boss of your money so you can make the most of your beautiful life.

Because when you see your money clearly, you can make choices.

Your future starts mattering more to you.

You trust yourself more.

With your money organized you can do bigger and better things with money. And with more money, you can live generously and enjoy all the good things life has to offer.

With your money on-purpose, you get to choose to live intentionally. And I can't wait to see what you choose to do with your money and that gorgeous life of yours.

Endnotes

1. Andrew Lisa, "23 Lottery Winners Who Lost Millions," GOBankingRates, https://www.gobankingrate s. com/net-worth/bankruptcy/lottery-winners-who-lost-mil-lions/.

2. Nicole Dow, "There's a 55% Chance You're Making This Money Mistake (but It's Easy to Fix)," The Penny Hoard-er, https://www.thepennyhoarder.com/budgeting/budgeting -statistics/. Sources vary, but this is the most conservative per-centage I was able to find. One source indicated that only 31% of households budget.

3. Jessica Dickler, "As Inflation Heats Up, 64% of Americans Are Now Living Paycheck to Paycheck," CNBC, https://w ww.cnbc.com/2022/03/08/as-prices-rise-64- percent-of-ameri-canslive-paycheck-to-paycheck.html.

4. Livia Gershon, "Budgeting Statistics: By the Numbers," CreditDonkey, https://www.creditdonkey.com/budgetingsta-tistics.html.

5. Elisa Ortiz, "Survey: How Many Americans Use a Budget?" Credit.com, https://www.credit.com/blog/budgeting-survey/.

6. Brad Klontz et al., Facilitating Financial Health, 2nd ed. (2016).

7. Erin Hurd and Lindsay Konsko, "Credit Cards Can Make You Spend More, but It's Not the Full Story," Nerd-Wallet, https://www.nerdwallet.com/ article/credit-cards/credit-cards-make-you-spend-more.

8. Cambridge Dictionary, https://dictionary.cambridge.org /dictionary/english/paradox.

9. Stephen Hawking, A Brief History of Time (2020).

10. Cambridge English Dictionary, https://dictionary.cambridge.org/us/dictionary/english/empowerment.

11. Charles Duhigg, *The Power of Habit* (2023).

12. J. G. Navarro, "Advertising Spending in the U.S. 2024," Statista, https://www.statista.com/statistics/272314/advertising-spending-in-the-us/.

13. Louise Story, "Anywhere the Eye Can See, It's Likely to See an Ad," The New York Times, https:// www.nytimes.com/2007/01/15/business/media/15everywhere.html.

14. Ibid.

15. James Clear, *Atomic Habits* (2018).

16. Matthew 7:20, *The Bible* (King James Version).

17. Holly Passalaqua and Mike Vulpo, "Johnny Depp's Former Business Managers Respond to Actor's $25 Million Lawsuit," E! Online, https://www.eonline.co m /news/825954/johnnydepp-s-former-business-managers-re-spond-to-actor-s-25million-lawsuit.

18. Rebecca Betterton, "Average Auto Loan Payments: What to Expect," Bankrate, https://www.bankrate.com/loans /auto-loans/average-monthly-car-payment/.

19. Chris Horymski, "Average Auto Loan Balance Increases to $22,612," Experian, https://www.experian.com/blogs/ask-experian/research/auto-loan-debt-study/.

20. U.S. Bureau of Labor Statistics, https://data.bls.gov/time-series/LNS14000000?years_option=all_years.

21. Samantha Delouya et al., "Binance Is the Latest Company Eyeing Job Cuts," Business Insider, https://www.businessinsi der.com/layoffs sweeping-the-us-these-are-the-companies-mak-ing-cuts-2023.

22. "Remarks by President Biden Announcing the Fiscal Year 2023 Budget," The White House, https://www.white house.gov/briefing-room/speeches-remarks/2022/03/28/re-marks-bypresident-biden-announcing-the-fiscal-year-2023-bud-get/.

23. William Green, *Richer, Wiser, Happier* (2021), 50.

24. Ibid., 178.

25. PYMTNS and Lending Club, "New Reality Check: The Paycheck-to-Paycheck Report," September 2022, https://www.pymnts.com/study/reality-check-paycheck-to-paycheck-consumer-planning-financial-emergency/.

26. Jade Scipioni, "Shaquille O'Neal After His Getting His First Million-Dollar Paycheck: What 'the Hell Is Fica'?" CNBC, https:// www.cnbc.com/2020/10/28/shaquille-oneal-ongetting-his-first-million-dollar-paycheck.html.

27. "The Time Shaquille O'Neal Spent $1 Million in One Day," Oprah's Master Class, https://www.youtube.com/watch?v=dbXHCvxpb1s.

28. Pablo Torre, "How (And Why) Athletes Go Broke," Sports Illustrated, https://vault.si.com/vault/2009/03/23/how-and-why-athletes-go-broke.

EMILY BURNETT is a writer, traveler, and principled dreamer actively building a life more her own. She finally came to trust herself with money, navigated her own debt-payoff journey, and writes in this book about money the way she wishes someone had talked to her about it.

In 2022, she left a decade-long tech career (her third unique career) to create more on her own terms. Since then, she's learned that meaningful work rarely follows a straight line, and that some dreams have to be risked and discovered their way into being.

Emily values faith, freedom and fun, likes talking with strangers wherever she travels, and considers herself at home in the western United States.

Thanks so much for reading *Dear Fellow Spender*. If this book resonated with you, I'd be very grateful if you'd leave a review on Amazon (scan below) or Goodreads. Your honest thoughts help others find this book and more financial and life hope and help.

For additional writings, find me on Substack at More to Your Life (moretoyour.life). This is where I share sometimes funny stories, travel mishaps, and personal essays about what makes life cool and people interesting.

Also, I love hearing from readers. Feel free to drop me a line at emilyburnett.me/books.

I'd spent more than a year exploring, traveling, and doing more than I'd ever done to create a life more my own. And it was time to put my thoughts about dreams—risking for them, persevering through apparent delays and dead-ends, maintaining hope—on paper.

Dear Fellow Dreamer: Waking Up, Taking Chances, and Creating A Life of Your Own is the result.

Equal parts inspirational, motivational, and practical, this book reads like a series of letters from one dreamer to another. Because that's exactly what it is. I intimately know the highs and lows of dreaming big and wrote this book for those who've ever had that feeling that there's just got to be more to life. There sure is.

Available now at emilyburnett.me/books.